SCEPTICISM, KNOWLEDGE, AND FORMS OF REASONING

Scepticism, Knowledge, and Forms of Reasoning

JOHN KOETHE

CORNELL UNIVERSITY PRESS

ITHACA AND LONDON

First published 2005 by Cornell University Press

Printed in the United States of America

Library of Congress Cataloging-in-Publication Data

Koethe, John.
     Scepticism, knowledge, and forms of reasoning / John Koethe.
        p. cm.
     Includes bibliographical references and index.
     ISBN-13: 978-0-8014-4432-6 (cloth : alk. paper)
     ISBN-10: 0-8014-4432-2 (cloth : alk. paper)
      1. Skepticism.   2. Knowledge, Theory of.   3. Epistemics.   4. Reasoning.
     I. Title.
     B837.K66 2005
     121—dc22

2005018411

Cornell University Press strives to use environmentally responsible suppliers and materials to the fullest extent possible in the publishing of its books. Such materials include vegetable-based, low-VOC inks and acid-free papers that are recycled, totally chlorine-free, or partly composed of nonwood fibers. For further information, visit our website at www.cornellpress.cornell.edu.

Cloth printing   10   9   8   7   6   5   4   3   2   1

❖

To my son,
John Robert

❖

CONTENTS

❖

PREFACE

Many years ago I tried to develop a version of the idea, which originates with Thompson Clarke, that there is nothing straightforwardly "wrong" with arguments for scepticism, arguments that embody patterns of reasoning about knowledge that we find unexceptional in everyday life. But I was not at all happy with the way that idea was developed then, and for several decades set scepticism aside while I pursued other philosophical interests. I started thinking about it again in the late 1990s, and the approach to scepticism and sceptical arguments presented in this book is the result of that renewed interest.

I am indebted to a number of people for discussions and suggestions, including William Demopoulos, Edward Hinchman, Mark Kaplan, Stephen Leeds, Julius Sensat, and two anonymous readers for Cornell University Press. And I owe a debt of long standing to the late Rogers Albritton, who originally sparked my interest in scepticism and directed my dissertation, and who helped sustain that interest, even at its lowest ebb, over the years.

J.K.

SCEPTICISM, KNOWLEDGE,
AND FORMS OF REASONING

❖

Introduction

Philosophical scepticism has been part of the landscape of Western philosophy for over two millennia, and its durability should, I believe, suggest that straightforward attempts at refutation or diagnosis are unlikely to be successful. There are three salient features of philosophical scepticism: first, it involves claims about our (lack of) knowledge that are drastically at odds with common sense, denying that one knows such things as that one is at a desk or that one has teeth; second, these claims are the conclusions of *arguments,* arrived at via inferences that purport to be valid from premises that purport to be true; and third, these sceptical claims are almost universally rejected, both by the man on the street and by philosophers engaged with scepticism (though for some philosophers this rejection takes the form of maintaining that the claims are technically correct though not, as they appear to be, at odds with common sense).[1] Given this, the problem of philosophical scepticism is not so much what to say about the view itself (there being a consensus that it should be rejected), but rather what to say about the arguments that purport to yield it. And since these arguments involve claims and principles concerning notions like knowledge and possibility, it is difficult to see how to explore the arguments without exploring these notions too.

The task of responding to scepticism can be seen as one of legitimating our common-sense convictions about knowledge, in the sense not of establishing the truth of those convictions (since they represent a default

1. This requires some qualification. Pyrrhonians of course endorsed scepticism, and among contemporary philosophers Peter Unger has too (see his *Ignorance: A Case for Scepticism* [Oxford: Oxford University Press, 1975]). Many positivists endorsed the claim that no empirical proposition can be known with certainty to be true, though they did not necessarily regard this as a sceptical claim.

1

position) but rather of providing an account of sceptical arguments that entitles us to persist in them in the face of those arguments. A straightforward response to scepticism would be to try to show that sceptical arguments are unsound, either because they involve an incorrect premise or assumption or because the inferences they involve are invalid. For instance, a familiar kind of sceptical argument adduces the mere possibility that one is, say, dreaming or a brain in a vat, and infers from this that one does not know, say, that one has teeth. Many philosophers have argued, on various grounds, that these alleged possibilities are not genuine ones; while others have denied, also on various grounds, that the admission of these outré possibilities is incompatible with our common-sense convictions about what we know.

What is striking, though, is the lack of consensus about these kinds of straightforward responses to scepticism. While each has its committed advocates, many if not most philosophers reject each particular response in favor of a different one, at the same time joining in the consensus that the conclusions of sceptical arguments should be rejected. The case is quite different with other long-standing philosophical issues. Consider the perennial disputes over realism, broadly speaking the view that the world has an objective character independent of our beliefs and theories about it which makes those beliefs and theories true or false. Philosophers are divided in their attitudes toward it, and I think it is safe to say that there is no consensus either in favor of or against realism in some form. But among those drawn to one side of the dispute or the other, there is a fair amount of agreement about what is wrong with arguments for the other side. Antirealists, for example, tend to accept the familiar criticisms of arguments for realism that appeal to the success of science, while those drawn to realism tend to agree about the fallacies in Berkeley's arguments for immaterialism. The fact that the consensus for rejecting scepticism is not mirrored in a consensus about what is wrong with the arguments for it is, I believe, a striking datum. It is, of course, a datum and not an argument. But I think it should at least lead us to question whether a straightforward response to scepticism and sceptical arguments is liable to succeed.

In the absence of a straightforward response to it, philosophical scepticism might be thought, as Stephen Shiffer suggests, to present a kind of paradox, in that reasoning that does not seem fallacious leads to conclusions inconsistent with propositions we regard as obviously true.[2] This

2. Stephen Shiffer, "Contextualist Solutions to Scepticism," *Proceedings of the Aristotelian Society* n.s. 96 (1996), 317–333.

way of regarding scepticism seems to me correct in a broad sense, though somewhat misleading and unspecific. In classical paradoxes like Russell's or the Liar, apparently self-evident principles (every nonvague predicate determines a class, every instance of the T-schema is true) are shown by reasoning that is uncontroversial to lead to contradictions; and the paradoxes are resolved by restricting the principles in various ways (though at the cost of forsaking their apparent obviousness). But in the case of philosophical scepticism, I believe that what is in question is the reasoning itself that leads to the unacceptable conclusions. Moreover, characterizing scepticism as paradoxical does nothing to legitimate the common-sense convictions about knowledge which it denies.

I think a better way of viewing scepticism is to see it as representing a conceptual anomaly involving an irresolvable tension between our practice of applying epistemic concepts like knowledge and the rules that, on reflection, seem to govern our application of and reasoning about those concepts. Our notion of valid reasoning depends on a certain equilibrium between our attitudes toward particular arguments or pieces of reasoning and toward the forms of reasoning those particular arguments embody. Yet there is no a priori guarantee that this equilibrium is bound to obtain, and the problem of scepticism arises, I want to argue, precisely because of the failure of this equilibrium between practice and reflection to obtain when the reasoning involves certain epistemic concepts. Philosophical scepticism thus presents a kind of conceptual anomaly analogous to, though considerably deeper than, Nelson Goodman's grue paradox.[3] But this tension between practice and reflection does not threaten our epistemic convictions, because those are ultimately made true by our practice of adhering to them, a practice that, as Hume observed, sceptical arguments are powerless to affect.

This is a broad—too broad—sketch of the account of scepticism I shall try to develop in this book, and I will offer a more detailed statement of it shortly. But let me first say a bit about the kinds of sceptical arguments that will be the focus of our concern. Most important are arguments of the dreaming or demon type, in which one begins by considering a proposition apparently known to be true (e.g., that I am sitting by the fire), formulates a sceptical hypothesis incompatible with that proposition (e.g., that I am falsely dreaming that I am sitting by the fire), argues that it is at least possible that this hypothesis is true, or that one does not know it to be false, and finally concludes that one does not know the proposition at issue to be true after all. On a familiar reconstruction of such arguments

3. Nelson Goodman, *Fact, Fiction, and Forecast* (Indianapolis: Bobbs-Merrill, 1965).

(though we will also consider an alternative interpretation), the inference involved appeals to a rule of inference I shall call the *transmission principle* (more commonly called the closure principle), which says that knowledge is transmitted by known logical consequence: if it is known that p_1, known that p_2, known that p_3, . . . , and it is also known that these logically entail q, then it follows that it is also known that q. Although our main concern will be with dreaming- and demon-type arguments, I shall also look at a number of other sceptical arguments, including what might be called the argument from error, which maintains that one's most carefully scrutinized beliefs no doubt include some false ones, and for all one knows, the belief under consideration may be one of the false ones. These additional sceptical arguments will not be pursued in detail, as I take dreaming-type arguments to be the most natural and compelling ones. But I want to bring out the fact that while its role in them may not be obvious, these other arguments appeal to the transmission principle too, so that the general question of the validity of sceptical arguments reduces to the question of the validity of that principle.

(This is an appropriate place to mention a kind of sceptical argument some philosophers consider important but that I shall not consider further, namely, the Pyrrhonian argument based on what Roderick Chisholm calls the problem of the criterion.[4] According to this argument, we can have knowledge only if we possess a general criterion for distinguishing true beliefs from those that merely seem true; but we can identify such a general criterion only by examining beliefs we genuinely know to be true. The apparent circularity here is supposed to lead to the conclusion that we cannot have genuine knowledge. It may be philosophical prejudice or blindness, but I have never found this argument particularly forceful. Anyone the least bit sympathetic to the claims of common sense, as I am, will simply reject the claim that knowing things requires the antecedent possession of the kind of general criterion this argument demands. One reason dreaming-type arguments are a staple of introductory philosophy courses is that the reasoning they involve can be made to seem so natural, a mere extension of a kind of reasoning we constantly employ outside the classroom. I do not think that the same can be said for the argument based on the problem of the criterion.)

The account of scepticism I shall offer incorporates and is facilitated by a treatment of the epistemic concepts of knowledge and possibility

---

4. Roderick Chisholm, *Theory of Knowledge* (Englewood Cliffs, N.J.: Prentice-Hall, 1966), chap. 4.

which, while it has points of contact with other philosophers' views of these notions, is perhaps sufficiently distinctive to warrant mention of some of its central elements here. One of these is the rejection of individual propositional knowledge as the basic concept of knowledge, in favor of the impersonal notion of knowledge's being *available* to the members of some relevant community. An individual knows that p if the knowledge that p is available (in his community) and he has, so to speak, availed himself of it, by coming to believe that p in a socially acceptable manner, one that would lead people to say of him that he knows that p. Epistemic possibility then turns out to be the dual of knowledge's being available: it is epistemically possible that p just in case the knowledge that not-p is not available, and the knowledge that p is available just in case it is not possible that not-p. One consequence of the duality of knowledge and possibility is that we cannot motivate a claim, say, that some sceptical hypothesis is not known to be false by appealing to the bare possibility of its truth, for to adduce that possibility is simply equivalent to maintaining that it is not known to be false.

A second element of my treatment of epistemic concepts is a rejection of what, to adapt Michael Williams's phrase,[5] I shall call *epistemological realism:* the view that there are facts, independent of our claims about knowledge and possibility, which make those claims true or false. On the alternative nonrealist view, claims about knowledge are made true or false by our socially sanctioned practices of making or rejecting them.[6] This is part of the reason sceptical arguments do not threaten the common-sense knowledge claims they are directed against, for while it is perhaps conceivable in some sense that our practices of endorsing such claims are alterable, the fact is that the challenge of philosophical scepticism has not succeeded in altering them. As should be clear from these remarks and those of the preceding paragraph, the treatment of epistemic concepts I shall propose is an inherently social one, and in support of it I shall suggest an account of the communicative role of terms like 'know' and 'possible.' Also, to forestall qualms about the coherence of this treatment of knowledge and possibility, I shall give a nonrealist semantics for these notions based on the topological operations of interior and closure.

5. Michael Williams, *Unnatural Doubts* (Cambridge: Basil Blackwell, 1991), 87–134.
6. Here I am following Michael Dummett's characterization of non- or antirealism, on which, roughly, it is not that propositions lack truth-conditions but rather that they are made true by the conditions under which we rationally accept them (see the writings of Dummett cited in note 3 of Chapter 4, where I shall discuss this further). Of course, for a knowledge claim to be true, the proposition said to be known has to be true.

Let me enter three brief disclaimers. First, my purpose is not so much to convince the reader of the truth of epistemological nonrealism as to show it to be a possible way of thinking about epistemic concepts and to bring out its relevance to the treatment of scepticism and sceptical arguments I shall offer. Second, while epistemological nonrealism and the allied account of epistemic concepts are part of the treatment of scepticism I want to propose, not all of their details are essential to that treatment, though I do think that they go together in a rather coherent way. Third, this account of knowledge and possibility is quite sketchy, and to defend it fully would require developing it in much more detail than I shall attempt here. I shall not try to offer the traditional sorts of analyses of these notions in terms of necessary and sufficient conditions (an enterprise about which I am dubious in any case) and then defend them against ingenious counterexamples. Rather, I shall say only enough to render this way of thinking about epistemic concepts plausible and to facilitate the presentation of the account of scepticism and sceptical arguments which is the main focus of this book.

I can now give a more detailed description of that account. A straightforward response to philosophical scepticism would either reject at least one of the premises of sceptical arguments or declare the inferences they involve invalid. In the case of dreaming-type arguments the crucial premise is that some sceptical hypothesis is possibly true or not known to be false (the premises of the other sceptical arguments we will look at being uncontroversial). But strategies for denying this premise have not proven successful. These include the kind of response offered by G. E. Moore, a kind of response often attributed to Wittgenstein, a coherentist response, and one supplied by the view called contextualism, which is probably the most influential current attempt to defuse sceptical arguments. Each of these has its adherents, but none of them has proven able to command a consensus—which is as it should be, because each of them is open to telling objections.

The second kind of straightforward response would reject as invalid the transmission principle that governs sceptical arguments. But this is not tenable either, since that principle is deeply embedded in our epistemic practices of making, challenging, and accepting knowledge claims, and of allowing that knowledge can be transmitted by deduction. The principle is implicit in those practices not in the sense that they conform to it exactly—the fact that we reject the sceptic's conclusions (even when we are unable to offer specific rebuttals of his premises) alone shows that—but in the sense that it provides the best (indeed, the only) explanation of those practices. Alternative explanations of why, for instance, knowledge is typically transmitted by deduction turn out to be unsatisfactory, and it does not seem possible to restrict the transmission principle in a way that filters out the "bad" (sceptical) inferences it licenses from the "good" ones we accept in everyday life. So given that we are unwilling and unable to alter those practices, the straightforward response of denying the validity of the sceptic's inferences is not open to us either.

This leaves us with the kind of conceptual anomaly I alluded to earlier: a certain rule of inference embedded in our epistemic practices leads to conclusions that in practice we reject. Philosophical scepticism thus represents a failure to achieve the kind of equilibrium between rules of inference we endorse and particular arguments or inferences we accept on which our notion of valid reasoning rests, for we are unwilling and unable to modify our attitudes toward either the rule or the inferences in the way needed to achieve this equilibrium. That is simply the way things stand with scepticism, for once we see what achieving this kind of fit between rules and arguments, reflection and practice, involves, we also see that there is no a priori guarantee that it will always be forthcoming, and no basis on which to criticize our failure to achieve it as irrational.

I have used the phrase "unwilling and unable" several times to characterize the alterability of our practices and attitudes in describing this response to scepticism, which might be called a descriptive account with normative consequences. It is descriptive in the sense that it is based on and accepts at face value our attitudes toward scepticism and sceptical arguments, both the attitudes of philosophers in finding attempts to deny the sceptic's premises unconvincing and the attitudes of the man on the street in countenancing everyday applications of the transmission principle while rejecting the sceptic's claims that are so at odds with common sense. But it has normative consequences, since there is no basis for criticizing these attitudes as irrational. In rejecting epistemological realism, we reject the idea that there are certain facts about knowledge to which our epistemic attitudes, practices, and claims should ultimately be held accountable. And there is no vantage point beyond our epistemic practices and our reflections on them from which we can demand that they be modified to achieve the kind of equilibrium between principles and inferences philosophical scepticism shows we have not attained. And since epistemic claims are ultimately made true by our settled acceptance of them, our persistence in the common-sense knowledge claims the sceptic demands we reject is perfectly legitimate, for not only are there no grounds on which this persistence can be criticized as irrational, the fact that we persist in them also makes them true.

Chapter 1 lays out a number of sceptical arguments and brings out the role the transmission plays in all of them. The most important of these are dreaming-type arguments, and so an alternative interpretation of these that does not appeal to the transmission principle will be considered and rejected, and the significance of the fact that our sceptical arguments are really argument-schemata will be made clear. Chapter 2 is a more or less self-contained examination of the concepts of knowledge and possibility. The evolution of the notion of epistemic possibility will be traced, along with its relation to individual propositional knowledge. The impersonal notion of knowledge's being available will then be introduced and shown to be the dual of epistemic possibility, and the chapter ends with an exploration of the inherently social character of knowledge. Chapter 3 takes up the first kind of straightforward response to scepticism, that of denying the truth of the sceptic's premise(s), in particular the claim that an appropriately formulated sceptical hypothesis is not known with certainty to be false. Moore's response to this claim will be discussed and criticized, as will a response sometimes attributed to Wittgenstein and a coherentist response. The chapter concludes with a more extended consideration of the currently influential account of sceptical arguments known as contextualism. Chapter 4 returns to the concepts of knowledge and possibility, arguing against the epistemologically realist view that holds that claims about them are answerable to facts that are independent of our acceptance or rejection of those claims. Part of that argument involves a proposal concerning the communicative role of epistemic terms which construes them in a way analogous to the way deflationists construe the role of the term 'true.' A nonrealist semantics for epistemic terms based on the topological operations of interior and closure will be offered, and in an appendix to the chapter this semantics will be used to frame a reply to the kind of general argument against realism put forward by Michael Dummett.[7]

Chapter 5 takes up the second kind of straightforward response to scepticism, that of denying the validity of the sceptic's inferences, inferences governed by the transmission principle. It will be argued that this principle is implicit and deeply embedded in our practices of making and

7. See the writings collected in *Truth and Other Enigmas* (Cambridge, Mass.: Harvard University Press, 1978), as well as his *Elements of Intuitionism* (Oxford: Oxford University Press, 1977), chap. 7, and "What Is a Theory of Meaning? (II)," in *Truth and Meaning*, ed. Gareth Evans and John McDowell (Oxford: Oxford University Press, 1976).

assessing knowledge claims and of treating knowledge as extendable through deduction. It will also be argued that alternative explanations of these practices are unsuccessful, and that the transmission principle cannot be restricted to avoid the unacceptable inferences the sceptic makes while allowing the acceptable ones we make in everyday life. The final chapter develops the view that scepticism represents a kind of conceptual anomaly having to do with a failure to attain a certain equilibrium between rules of inference and the actual inferences we make, and tries to identify what it is about the concept of knowledge that gives rise to this anomaly. The suggestion that there are other concepts that share these features and give rise to similar anomalies is explored in brief discussions of the problems of moral luck and human freedom, and the book concludes with some reflections on agreement and generality.

CHAPTER ONE

Sceptical Arguments and the
Transmission Principle

Philosophical scepticism has at least two distinctive features. While sober reflection on human fallibility and our tendency to leap to conclusions might suggest that the extent of our knowledge of the world is somewhat more limited than we may initially take it to be, philosophical scepticism maintains that the extent of this knowledge is either nonexistent or *radically* more limited than we take it, even after critical reflection, to be. Second, this contention is the result of an *argument* (or the repeated applications of a form of argument), an argument that, whether or not it can ultimately withstand scrutiny, has at least an initial air of plausibility. In this chapter I want to inventory some of the leading arguments for scepticism, and try to bring out the role played in them by a certain principle regarding knowledge and inference. In subsequent chapters I shall assess these arguments, focusing mostly on the kind of argument Descartes adduces in the First Meditation. My concern here is simply with how sceptical arguments should be understood or reconstructed: what are the forms of such arguments, what principles license the inferences they involve, and what is the significance of the fact that they are really argument-schemata, which have to be instantiated to yield actual arguments? I would not want to claim that this inventory covers all sceptical arguments of philosophical interest. But I do think that the ones to be discussed here are among the most compelling and important.

1. Dreaming-type Arguments

The classical form of sceptical argument is that of the argument adduced by Descartes in the First Meditation. The passage is one of the most familiar in Western philosophy, but since it will be useful to have it before us, I shall quote it here. He is considering his belief that he is at present sitting in front of a fire, and writes:

> Nevertheless, I must remember that I am a man, and that consequently I am accustomed to sleep and in my dreams to imagine the same things that lunatics imagine when awake, or sometimes things which are even less plausible. How many times has it occurred that the quiet of the night made me dream of my usual habits: that I was here, clothed in a dressing gown, and sitting by the fire, although I was in fact lying undressed in bed! It seems apparent to me now, that I am not looking at this paper with my eyes closed, that this head that I shake is not drugged with sleep, that it is with design and deliberate intent that I stretch out this hand and perceive it. What happens in sleep seems not at all as clear and distinct as all this. But I am speaking as though I never recall having been misled, while asleep, by similar illusions. When I consider these matters carefully, I realise so clearly that there are no conclusive indications by which waking life can be distinguished from sleep that I am quite astonished, and my bewilderment is such that it is almost able to convince me that I am sleeping.[1]

The form of the argument seems to be as follows (later I shall discuss another reconstruction of the argument): one selects a proposition p (here, I am sitting by the fire) representative of those one takes one's self to know with certainty to be true. Next one formulates a *sceptical hypothesis* along these lines:

> SH P is actually false, but it *seems* to me exactly as though p were true— that is, I am having all the subjective thoughts, sensations, feelings, apparent memories, and so on that I would expect to have if p were true.

In the dreaming argument the sceptical hypothesis is fleshed out with the supposition that a vivid dream is making it seem to one that p is true; in the demon argument this is due to the machinations of a powerful demon controlling one's thoughts and experiences; in a contemporary variation it is because one is really a brain in a vat being manipulated by alien sci-

1. René Descartes, *Meditations on First Philosophy*, in *The Philosophical Works of Descartes*, ed. Elizabeth S. Haldane and G. R. T. Ross, vol. 1 (Cambridge: Cambridge University Press, 1968), 145–146.

entists; and many other scenarios are conceivable. Part of the sceptical hypothesis, on this reconstruction of the argument, is that p is *false* (Descartes imagines that rather than being by the fire he is actually *in bed*, and he speaks of being *misled* by dreams, and of their presenting *illusions*; and in the demon argument the evil genius employs his energies in *deceiving* him); hence if p is true, then SH must be false. But on reflection he must admit that he does not *know* SH to be false, since there are no "conclusive indications" of waking life that would enable him to refute it. The conclusion is then that he does not, after all, know p to be true:

    (1) If p is true, then SH is false.
    (2) I don't know that SH is false.

    ———

    (3) I don't know that p is true.

What licenses the inference from (1) and (2) to (3)? Since ¬SH is a logical consequence of p, a principle to the effect that if one knows that p, then one knows p's logical consequences (and hence if one fails to know a logical consequence of p, one does not know that p) would, if valid, license it. Such a principle is clearly unacceptable, though: it would, for instance, make knowledge of Peano's axioms sufficient for arithmetical omniscience. But since the fact that ¬SH follows logically from p is obvious, we can appeal to the weaker, and seemingly plausible, principle that if one knows that p, then one also knows to be true those propositions one *knows* to be consequences of p (and hence if one fails to know something one knows to be a logical consequence of p, one does not know that p):

    $[Kp, K(p \vdash q)] \vdash Kq$.[2]

Since according to this principle knowledge is closed under known logical consequence, it is commonly called the *closure principle.* I prefer to call it the *transmission principle* to emphasize its role in the production of new knowledge by drawing out the consequences of things already known.[3] Stated in full generality as a rule of inference, it reads:

    (T) $[Kp_1, Kp_2, \ldots, Kp_n, K(p_1, p_2, \ldots, p_n \vdash q)] \vdash Kq$.

---

    2. For reasons to be explained in the next chapter, I have not indexed the operator K to individuals. For present purposes, though, take this index to be understood.

    3. Crispin Wright, in "Scepticism and Dreaming: Imploding the Demon," *Mind* 100 (1991), 87–116 (a work I shall discuss later), calls the principle that available warrant is transmitted by logical consequence 'Transmission.'

From (T) we can obtain the rule

(T') $[K(p_1, p_2, \ldots, p_n \vdash q), \neg Kq] \vdash \neg Kp_1 \lor \neg Kp_2 \lor \ldots \lor \neg Kp_n$,

which is the form in which the transmission principle figures in sceptical arguments of the dreaming type.

Let me clarify the status of the transmission principle. A question to be addressed later, in Chapter 5, is whether or not it is valid. It is not of course a valid schema of standard first-order logic, but the question is whether if we extend standard logic by treating K as a logical term, (T) is a valid rule of this extended "epistemic" logic. I think it is also important that (T) be construed as a rule of inference, rather than as a substantive (schematic) general principle to the effect that if certain propositions are known to be true, then if it is also known that those propositions are true then so is q, q is also known. Of course, given the deduction theorem, we can move back and forth between treating the transmission principle as a rule of inference and as a substantive generalization involving conditionals, but there are at least two reasons for treating it in the former way.

The first, and least important, is that this seems more faithful to the phenomenology, so to speak, of sceptical arguments. One is invited to *conclude* that if one knows, say, that one is by the fire, one must know that one is not dreaming; and having then conceded that one can't know this, one then *infers* that one doesn't know that a fire is nearby either. (T) is meant to codify the reasoning involved in those inferences. An alternative reconstruction of sceptical arguments would treat them as enthymematic, with a substantive generalization about knowledge as a suppressed premise. It seems to me implausible that students in introductory philosophy, for instance, can be brought to see the cogency of sceptical reasoning because they already implicitly accept such a substantive general principle.

The second and more important reason is that treating the transmission principle as a rule of inference facilitates the presentation of the account of the persistence of scepticism I want to offer—namely, that it represents a failure to attain a certain kind of mesh between actual inferences concerning knowledge we accept or reject in practice and the rules of inference governing those inferences. If we treat the transmission principle as a substantive generalization, at the end of the day we will be left with a number of intuitively plausible claims and principles about knowledge which are mutually inconsistent, but without an account or diagnosis of why this inconsistency arises and whether or how it can be eliminated by fine-tuning our intuitions. Treating it as a rule of inference, on the other hand, allows us to diagnose the clash of intuitions concerning knowledge and sceptical arguments in a way that entitles us to reject the conclusions of those arguments without identifying some straightforward fallacy in them—or so I hope to show.

The role of the closure or transmission principle in dreaming-type arguments is of course well known.[4] Less obvious, however, is its role in other kinds of sceptical arguments.

2. Some Other Sceptical Arguments

Another form of sceptical argument might be called the argument from fallibility. It begins by asking us to consider all those propositions (or alternatively, all those propositions of a certain kind or with a certain subject matter) that have met whatever standards of epistemic scrutiny we deem appropriate for knowledge, and are in this sense on an epistemic par. It should be remarked that this notion of epistemic parity is an internalist one, since it is something we are assumed to be able, in principle, to ascertain. The argument proceeds by asserting that, on reflection, for all we know there are a few falsehoods among these propositions: that is, that we don't really know for certain that there aren't one or more falsehoods among the propositions that have withstood our strictest scrutiny and are thus on an epistemic par (indeed, given the reality of human fallibility, it seems overwhelmingly likely that there *are* falsehoods among them). It is then inferred that we do not know to be true each of these surviving propositions. Considering a particular proposition that has withstood our strictest scrutiny, we then draw the conclusion that for all we know it is false, or in other words not a proposition we know to be true. Here is the argument stated in the singular first person:

(1) All the propositions that have survived my strictest scrutiny are on an epistemic par.
(2) But for all I know, there are falsehoods among these propositions (that is, I don't know that there aren't falsehoods among them).
(3) So I don't know to be true each of these propositions.

4. See, for instance, Robert Nozick, *Philosophical Explanations* (Cambridge, Mass.: Harvard University Press, 1981), 167–228, and Jonathan Dancy, *Introduction to Contemporary Epistemology* (Oxford: Basil Blackwell, 1985), 7–22.

(4) P (e.g., I'm sitting by a fire) is one such proposition, on an epistemic par with all the others.

---

(5) For all I know, p is a falsehood—that is, I don't know that p.

In this argument the role of the transmission principle is in the inference from (2) to (3). Let $p_1, p_2, \ldots, p_n$ be the propositions that have withstood whatever degree of scrutiny is deemed necessary for knowledge and so are on an epistemic par. (2) says that for all I know, some of $p_1, p_2, \ldots, p_n$ are false, that is, $\neg K \neg (\neg p_1 \vee \neg p_2 \vee \ldots \vee \neg p_n)$, or equivalently $\neg K(p_1 \wedge p_2 \wedge \ldots \wedge p_n)$. The principle that if one knows a number of propositions to be true one also knows their conjunction to be true is a consequence of the transmission principle, which, in the form of (T'), allows us to infer that I don't know that p_1 or I don't know that $p_2 \ldots$ or I don't know that p_n.

The inference from (4) to (5) does not directly involve the transmission principle but rather appeals to the notion of epistemic parity: since the particular proposition p under consideration does not differ in any epistemically relevant respect from the others referred to in (3), some of which are not known to be true, there seems to be no basis for maintaining that it is known to be true while some of the others are not. Though externalists may be tempted to balk at this step, such an objection would be misguided. To see why, consider a weaker version of the argument from fallibility, which replaces (2) with

(2') There are falsehoods among these propositions.

This argument is weaker than the original version in two respects. First, (2'), though no doubt true, is a stronger claim than (2). But more important, the new version *is* open to objection by externalists. In the new version the inference from (2) to (3) does not appeal to the transmission principle but follows directly from the principle that knowledge entails truth. But the inference from (4) to

(5') For all I know, p is one of the false ones—that is, I don't know that p.

is now problematic, since an externalist can insist that only those propositions among those which have withstood scrutiny which are actually false are not known to be true; those which have withstood scrutiny which are true are known to be so. But this objection does not apply to the original version, since in it the basis for (3) is not the claim that some of the surviving propositions are actually false but rather the weaker claim that it is not known that there are no falsehoods among them, a claim compatible with their all being true. Thus the externalist cannot maintain that the propositions which, according to (3), are not known to be true are limited to those which are actually false, since none of them may be false.[5] The source of the failure of some of them to be known must lie elsewhere, and since all are on a par epistemically, if some are not known to be true, it is tempting to conclude that none are, and that in particular p is not.

Another sceptical argument is one attributed to Saul Kripke.[6] Again, we are asked to consider a proposition we are confident we know to be true. We are then reminded that if this proposition is true, it follows that any apparent evidence against it that might arise must be misleading evidence. So if we know the proposition to be true, do we not know that any apparent evidence against it will be misleading evidence that should be disregarded? But surely, the argument proceeds, we should never disregard apparent evidence against a proposition we take to be true, since we cannot know, without further investigation, that such apparent evidence *is* misleading. Therefore we do not really know that the proposition is true:

(1) If p (e.g., I'm sitting by a fire) is true, then any apparent evidence that might arise against it will be evidence for something false, and thus misleading evidence.

(2) If I know p to be true, then I know that any apparent evidence against it that might arise will be misleading evidence that should be disregarded.

(3) But I don't know that any apparent evidence against p that might arise will be misleading evidence, and I shouldn't automatically disregard it.

———

(4) I don't know p to be true.

In this argument the replacement for $p_1, p_2, \ldots, p_n$ in the transmission principle is the particular proposition under consideration, and the replacement for q is the proposition that any apparent evidence against that proposition that might arise will be misleading evidence. The transmis-

5. Of course, externalists like Nozick may reject the transmission principle itself. I shall discuss its status in Chapter 5.

6. See Gilbert Harman, *Thought* (Princeton: Princeton University Press, 1973), 148.

sion principle then licenses the inference from (1) to (2) (the admonition in (2) to disregard the apparent evidence seems warranted by the supposition that I *know* it to be misleading evidence, which according to the transmission principle I do know if I know the proposition under consideration to be true).

In all the sceptical arguments discussed so far a crucial premise is that some proposition—the one substituted for q in the transmission principle—is not *known* to be true: it is not known that the sceptical hypothesis is false, it is not known that there aren't some falsehoods among the propositions that have survived scrutiny, it is not known that any apparent evidence against p will be misleading evidence. It might be thought that to some or all of these arguments there correspond additional and different arguments in which the crucial premise is that something is epistemically *possible:* there is a possibility that the sceptical hypothesis is true, or that there are falsehoods among our carefully scrutinized beliefs, or that genuine evidence against p will arise. These additional arguments "from possibility" may seem to some more compelling than those we have discussed: some may be more inclined to grant, say, that there is some *possibility,* however remote, that one is now dreaming, than that I don't know that I am not; and there have been many philosophers who have maintained that no empirical proposition is ever absolutely certain, in that there is always some possibility that it will turn out to be false.[7] On the other hand, some may find them weaker, for there are those who maintain that there are perfectly literal senses of the word "know" in which knowing something to be true is compatible with there being a theoretical possibility of its being false. In either case, such arguments would appear to appeal to principles different from, though parallel to, the transmission principle, principles governing epistemic possibility rather than knowledge. For instance, instead of (T'), an argument from possibility of the dreaming type might be thought to appeal to principles like

(T'') $[K(p_1, p_2, \ldots, p_n \vdash q), P\neg q] \vdash P\neg p_1 \vee P\neg p_2 \vee \ldots \vee P\neg p_n$

or

(T''') $[K(p_1, p_2, \ldots, p_n \vdash q), P\neg q] \vdash \neg Kp_1 \vee \neg Kp_2 \ldots \vee \neg Kp_n.$

7. See the discussion of what Norman Malcolm called 'The Verification Argument' in section 1 of the next chapter.

(Restricted to a single proposition, (T''') expresses the familiar idea that in order to know a proposition to be true, one must be able to rule out every known counterpossibility to its truth.)

But I do not think that the contemplated sceptical arguments from possibility differ at all from the arguments we have already considered, for I think that (T'), (T''), and (T''') are really the same principle (along with (T), of course). In the next chapter I shall discuss the concepts of knowledge and possibility and the relations between them, and I will argue that knowledge and possibility are best thought of as *duals:* a proposition is known to be true (Kp) if and only if there is no possibility that it is false ($\neg P \neg p$), and it is possible that a proposition is true (Pp) if and only if it is not known to be false ($\neg K \neg p$). No doubt this sounds strange, for while epistemic possibility seems like an impersonal notion, it is common to take the fundamental concept of knowledge to be that of individual or personal knowledge. But let me defer further discussion of these issues until the next chapter.

3. An Alternative Reconstruction of Dreaming-type Arguments

In "Certainty" G. E. Moore recounts a story about "a well-known Duke of Devonshire ... [who] once dreamt that he was speaking in the House of Lords and, when he woke up, found that he *was* speaking in the House of Lords."[8] The inclination is surely strong to say that although the dozing duke's assessment of his circumstances was not incorrect, he did not, prior to awakening, know himself to be in those circumstances. My earlier reconstruction of the type of sceptical argument exemplified by the dreaming and demon arguments involves a sceptical hypothesis to the effect that the belief under consideration is *mistaken,* a hypothesis one does not know to be false—and hence, via the transmission principle, one does not know the belief to be true. But the Duke of Devonshire in Moore's anecdote is not mistaken in his belief that he is speaking in the House of Lords, and yet apparently does not know that he is. This suggests an alternative reconstruction of dreaming-type arguments, one in which the transmission principle plays no role.

Barry Stroud and Crispin Wright offer just such an interpretation of these arguments.[9] The first step in this interpretation alleges an incom-

8. G. E. Moore, "Certainty," in *Philosophical Papers* (New York: Collier, 1962), 241.
9. Barry Stroud, *The Significance of Philosophical Scepticism* (Oxford: Oxford University Press, 1984), 9–24, and Wright, "Scepticism and Dreaming," 91.

patibility between my knowing the proposition p under consideration and my presently dreaming (whether veridically or not), or being under the influence of a powerful demon (who may or may not be deceiving me), or whatnot:

(1) If I know that p, then I am not presently dreaming.

As before, the second step alleges that I do not know that I am not in the condition supposedly incompatible with knowing that p:

(2) I don't know that I am not presently dreaming.

How is it supposed to follow from (1) and (2) that I do not know that p? Stroud proposes, though says little to motivate, a principle that Wright dubs *Descartes' principle:*

(D) If one knows that p, one must know to be satisfied any condition that one knows to be necessary for knowing that p.[10]

Given (D), together with the assumption that I realize that my not presently dreaming is a necessary condition for my knowing that p, the sceptical conclusion follows:

(3) I don't know that p.

One important difference between this reconstruction of the argument and the earlier one involving the transmission principle is worth pointing out immediately. In the earlier reconstruction both p and the sceptical hypothesis SH were proposition *schemata* rather than particular propositions, and the necessary condition for knowing that p—knowing SH to be false—varied with the proposition instantiating p. On Stroud's and Wright's reconstruction only p is schematic, and the alleged necessary condition for knowing that p—for example, that I am not presently dreaming—is expressed by a particular proposition that is the same regardless of the proposition instantiating p. In other words, their interpretation alleges some particular condition (initially, that I'm not dreaming, but whose exact formulation, as we shall see, is a matter of some difficulty) necessary for knowing any proposition (or perhaps any proposition of a certain kind) to be true.

10. Stroud, *Significance of Philosophical Scepticism,* 29, and Wright, "Dreaming and Scepticism," 91.

Two questions arise at this point. First, what proposition expresses the alleged necessary condition for knowing that p, and *is* it actually a necessary condition? Second, does Descartes' principle (D) furnish the basis for a cogent sceptical argument?

As regards the first question, although the inference from

(1) I am now dreaming

to, say,

(2) I don't know that I'm sitting by the fire

may at first seem immediate and compelling, a strategy once used by Roderick Chisholm to cast doubt on a kind of entailment alleged to hold by C. I. Lewis may be employed here to call it into question.[11] Lewis had claimed that any material object statement entailed a large number of "terminating judgements" referring only to immediate sensory experience. Chisholm pointed out that if so, the entailment must still hold when the material object statement is conjoined with any other proposition with which it is compatible. But it is easy to find propositions that, conjoined with the material object statement, would lead us to infer the negation of the terminating judgment in question, or at least seem to block the supposed entailment. The same seems true here. As the story of the Duke of Devonshire indicates, it is certainly possible for some beliefs entertained in the course of a dream to be true, and there is no logical impossibility in the thought of highly reliable dreams, dreams in which an overwhelming majority of the beliefs arising in their course are true. And there is no logical impossibility in this fact about the reliability of dreams being generally known. And if we conjoin (1) with a proposition consistent with it,

(3) Dreams are generally known to be highly reliable processes giving rise to beliefs almost all of which are true,

the temptation to infer (2) from the conjunction of (1) and (3) is significantly lessened if not entirely dispelled—which casts considerable doubt on the claim that (2) follows from (1) alone. And a similar strategy can be used to call into question comparable inferences involving demons, brains in vats, and so on.[12]

11. Roderick Chisholm, "The Problem of Empiricism," in *Perceiving, Sensing, and Knowing*, ed. Robert J. Swartz (New York: Doubleday, 1965), 347–354.
12. I should emphasize that my purpose is to criticize a reconstruction of dreaming-

Wright claims that it is a conceptual truth about knowledge that a necessary condition for a belief's qualifying as knowledge is that it have a suitable causal etiology, and that dreaming is an example of a process incompatible with the requisite etiology.[13] In Chapter 4 I shall propose an account of knowledge on which the *only* necessary (though of course not sufficient) condition for knowing that p is p itself.[14] But for the present, the preceding argument should lead us to question whether an absence of *dreaming* is actually part of the causal etiology required, according to Wright, for knowledge. Wright seems to recognize this, and proposes to capture the alleged necessary condition for knowledge generally by trying to characterize a state that subsumes dreaming and "necessarily precludes the causal conditions for perception but, in addition, likewise precludes the causal conditions for competent intellection," a state he calls *maundering*.[15] If a person is maundering, he is aware of "phenomenologically smooth" successions of experiences, mental episodes, items, and other introspectibilia which are indistinguishable from those involved in genuine perceiving and thinking but which "have an aetiology inconsistent with their being genuinely intellective/perceptual."[16] Any beliefs one has while maundering (and Wright seems to allow for maundering beliefs), whatever their content or apparent content, will not qualify as knowledge, or even as warranted. The absence of maundering is to be a necessary condition for knowledge generally, and is meant to capture what is gestured at in the requirement that one not be dreaming, in the grip of a demon, a brain in a vat, and so on.

Let us assume for the sake of argument—but only for the sake of argument—that an absence of maundering is a necessary condition for knowledge generally, and turn to the second question, the question whether this supposition, together with Descartes' principle (D), enables

---

type arguments offered by Stroud and Wright, not to examine in detail their discussions of those arguments. But in fairness to Stroud, it should be noted that he holds that knowing that one is not dreaming is a necessary condition for knowing something *on the basis of the senses* or *by perception* (*Significance of Philosophical Scepticism*, 23). I do not think that subdividing knowledge into various species, each with its own necessary conditions, affects the overall point of my criticism, but I shall not pursue the matter here.

13. For reasons indicated below, Wright prefers to cast his discussion of scepticism in terms of warrant rather than knowledge. For reasons I also indicate below, I prefer to continue to cast it in terms of knowledge, and have reformulated Wright's claims to apply to knowledge.

14. More precisely, the proposal will be that p is the only necessary condition for the knowledge that p's being *available*, a notion to be introduced in the next chapter.

15. Wright, "Dreaming and Scepticism," 106.

16. Ibid.

us to formulate a cogent sceptical argument, one not involving the transmission principle. I want to draw on aspects of Wright's discussion of the envisaged sort of argument to argue that the answer to this question is no; but first I need to say something about the framework and focus of his discussion, which differ from those of the present one.

Wright believes that sceptical arguments that yield conclusions to the effect that we do not actually know certain things common sense takes us to know are of little significance, since they simply invite a concession he calls the *Russellian retreat:* that while we do not strictly *know* these things, we nevertheless are fully justified in believing them.[17] Since he takes this to be a concession we can comfortably live with, he maintains that to be genuinely troubling, a sceptical argument must yield the conclusion that we are not even justified in believing things common sense takes us to know and to be justified in believing; and he introduces a notion of warrant which he takes to conform to (an analogue of) Descartes' principle (D), and which enables him to construct analogues of dreaming-type arguments framed in terms of warrant rather than knowledge. As I made clear earlier, and shall emphasize again later, a conclusion to the effect that I don't, strictly speaking, know, for instance, that I have teeth, *does* seem to me to be intolerable and an insult to common sense, in that it denies something I claim to be perfectly *obvious.* Thus I shall continue to cast the discussion in terms of knowledge.

One other preliminary point concerns the status of Descartes' principle (D), which we can write as

$$(D) \quad K(Kp \rightarrow q) \rightarrow (Kp \rightarrow Kq)$$

or

$$(D') \quad K(Kp \rightarrow q) \rightarrow (\neg Kq \rightarrow \neg Kp).$$

This is a strong claim, which, as Wright notes, is liable to be objected to by externalists, who would argue that even if, for instance, we know that knowing that p requires us to stand in some suitable relation involving reliability of belief to the external world, there is no reason to require us to be aware that or know that we do stand in such a relation. Nevertheless, let us also grant the principle for the sake of argument, along with

---

17. Ibid., 88, and Bertrand Russell, *The Problems of Philosophy* (Oxford: Oxford University Press, 1912), chaps. 1 and 2.

the assumption that an absence of maundering, ¬M, is a necessary condition for knowledge.

We then have the following version of a dreaming-type argument:

(1) $K(Kp \rightarrow \neg M)$
(2) $\neg K \neg M$
___
(3) $\neg Kp$

Assuming the validity of (D′) and the necessity of the absence of maundering for knowledge, this argument is valid and the first premise (1) is true.[18]

The problem, though, is that such an argument cannot possibly be successful, for it is easy to show that premises (1) and (2), together with our other assumptions, are inconsistent. To see why, simply instantiate p in (D) by $Kp \rightarrow \neg M$, and q, as before, by $\neg M$:[19]

$$K(K(Kp \rightarrow \neg M) \rightarrow \neg M) \rightarrow (K(Kp \rightarrow \neg M) \rightarrow K \neg M).$$

If ¬M is, as we are assuming, known to be a necessary condition for knowing anything, including that $Kp \rightarrow \neg M$, then the antecedent of this is true and so

$$K(Kp \rightarrow \neg M) \rightarrow K \neg M.$$

But the antecedent of this is just premise (1), and the consequent the denial of premise (2). So if ¬M is a necessary condition for knowledge and Descartes′ principle is valid, premises (1) and (2) cannot both be true.

It might be thought that the difficulty can be avoided if we replace (D) with

(D*) $(Kp \rightarrow q) \rightarrow (Kp \rightarrow Kq)$

or

(D*′) $(Kp \rightarrow q) \rightarrow (\neg Kq \rightarrow \neg Kp)$,

---

18. Since maundering is incompatible with knowledge even of conceptual truths, (1) holds for all p.
19. See note 12.

requiring any necessary condition for knowledge, whether known to be so or not, to be known, and then deploying this modified sceptical argument:

(1*) $Kp \rightarrow \neg M$
(2) $\neg K \neg M$
___
(3) $\neg Kp$

But the revised principle (D*) would seem even more objectionable to externalists since it requires us to know to be satisfied *all* necessary conditions for knowledge, even those we have no idea *are* necessary conditions. Worse, it would, for example, confer arithmetical omniscience on anyone with a knowledge of Peano's axioms, since q could be any consequence of p (and hence of Kp), whether known to be one or not. And finally, even the revised argument cannot be successfully adduced. Once again, instantiate p by $Kp \rightarrow \neg M$ and q by $\neg M$:

$$(K(Kp \rightarrow \neg M) \rightarrow \neg M) \rightarrow (\neg K \neg M \rightarrow \neg K(Kp \rightarrow \neg M)).$$

If $\neg M$ is a necessary condition for knowledge, the antecedent is true and so

$$\neg K \neg M \rightarrow \neg K(Kp \rightarrow \neg M).$$

But here the antecedent is just premise (2), and the consequent is the denial that premise (1*) is known to be true. So if $\neg M$ is a necessary condition for knowledge and (D*) is valid, then either the first premise of the new argument can never be known to be true or the second premise is false.

Thus no cogent sceptical argument along the lines of Stroud's and Wright's proposed reconstruction of dreaming-type arguments seems to be forthcoming. Wright actually arrives at similar conclusions regarding the premises of the sceptical arguments framed in terms of warrant he considers, but since he takes these to be *correct* interpretations of dreaming-type arguments, he sees these conclusions as amounting to a (limited) refutation of scepticism.[20] My own assessment is that these conclusions about the premises of the proposed arguments show them to be unsatis-

---

20. Wright, "Dreaming and Scepticism," 114–115.

factory reconstructions of classical dreaming-type arguments, by contrast with reconstructions based on the transmission principle.[21]

4. Sceptical Arguments as Schematic

At the beginning of this chapter I said that philosophical scepticism has two distinctive features: it maintains that the extent of our knowledge of the world is radically less than it seems obviously to be, and that this contention is the conclusion of an argument, or of the repeated applications of a form of argument. The reason for the latter qualification is that all the sceptical arguments we have considered are actually argument-*schemata*. Instantiating the schematic letter p yields particular arguments, each one for the conclusion that I do not know some particular thing: that I have teeth, that my name is 'John,' that I teach philosophy, that I have two cats, and so on. Although the fact that the instantiated propositions are presumably representative of many other propositions of their general kinds invites us to generalize these conclusions, none of the instantiated argument-schemata are direct arguments for a sweeping conclusion to the effect that we know nothing, or next to nothing, about the external world. Of course, by repeatedly instantiating one of our argument-schemata by propositions we believe to be true of the external world, we can arrive at a large number of claims that, conjoined with claims about what propositions would have to be included in the range of any knowledge we might have of the external world, imply such a sweeping conclusion. But the fact remains that dreaming-type arguments, and the others we have considered, do not, by themselves, yield this conclusion directly.

This is significant for several reasons. First, the fact that these arguments yield conclusions to the effect that one does not know particular things one takes one's self to know, rather than something more sweeping, influences our likely response to philosophical scepticism. Given an argument for *global scepticism*—the thesis, in (for instance) Peter Klein's formulation, that "none of the beliefs about the external world, though coherent with other such beliefs, is knowledge"[22]—one is likely to focus on the philosophical significance of the conclusion itself: to find it, as did

---

21. I will note yet another reconstruction of dreaming-type arguments in Chapter 3 in connection with contextualism.

22. Peter Klein, "Radical Interpretation and Global Skepticism," in *Truth and Interpretation: Perspectives on the Philosophy of Donald Davidson*, ed. Ernest LePore (Oxford: Basil Blackwell, 1986), 374.

the Pyrrhonians, conducive to a kind of serenity brought about by a sus-pension of doxastic commitments; to see it, as does Stanley Cavell, as a source of anxiety at the prospect of an estrangement from the world;[23] to respond to it, as does Michael Williams, by rejecting the foundationalism he takes to lead to it.[24] Or it may seem to invite Wright's Russellian re-sponse, for as a broad and abstract claim with no obvious practical sig-nificance for our lives, it is easy to suppose that the sort of knowledge of the world it denies we have is something we can live without.

But the particular denials of knowledge that our sceptical arguments yield—that I don't know that my name is 'John,' that I don't know that I have two cats, and so on—are of no *inherent* philosophical significance. There could perfectly well be circumstances—a sudden spell of amnesia, a break-in by catnappers after I left home this morning—in which the claims that I don't know such things are of no philosophical interest at all. Yet the fact that they are not inherently significant does not mean that they are devoid of philosophical significance. I am reluctant to say that their significance lies in the fact that they are at odds with common sense, for the phrase "common sense" may suggest a distinctive and privileged source of beliefs, or a distinctive and privileged kind of belief; and in that sense of "common sense," common sense is not something I would want to appeal to or defend. I prefer to say that what makes these claims of philosophical significance is, first, the fact that, given circumstances as they are, not only are such things as that my name is 'John' and that I have two cats *obvious,* it is also obvious that they are things I *know.* Focusing on particular sceptical claims like these invites the philosophical reflection, it seems to me, that they are obviously false, and makes the Russellian re-treat seem absurd. Another source of their significance lies in the fact that they are the result of *reasoning,* reasoning that, while we have yet to as-sess it, is not *obviously* defective, certainly not as obviously defective as its conclusions are obviously false. This fact tends to concentrate our re-sponse to scepticism on the reasoning that leads to such patently false conclusions rather than on the content of those conclusions; and to me the philosophical significance of scepticism lies not so much in what it may or may not suggest about our relation to the world, but rather in what it may show about reasoning, arguments, and inference. That an obviously false conclusion could seem to follow from a line of reasoning that does

23. Stanley Cavell, *In Quest of the Ordinary* (Chicago: University of Chicago Press, 1988), 4.
24. Michael Williams, *Unnatural Doubts* (Cambridge: Basil Blackwell, 1991), 51–56.

not seem obviously defective calls into question the character and status of that reasoning, and of reasoning in general. While we may also respond to global scepticism by focusing on the nature and status of the reasoning that leads to it, in the case of reasoning that leads to such local conclusions as that I don't know that I have teeth, there is little else to focus on.

A second reason that the fact that our sceptical arguments are schematic is significant has to do with what constitutes a satisfactory refutation or diagnosis of philosophical scepticism. Yielding as they do local, particularized denials of knowledge, they are not open to what might be called *global* refutations of scepticism. For instance, Williams maintains that scepticism rests on an assumption of foundationalism, and if the latter is rejected, the case for scepticism collapses. Now perhaps there are sceptical arguments that do involve some sort of foundationalist premise— Hume's argument concerning induction might be one such since it involves an assumption about how propositions of different kinds can be established or justified. But since dreaming-type arguments (as well as the others) make no explicit appeal to foundationalism, or to any other theory of justification, it is hard to see how criticisms of foundationalism are relevant to them. It may be that what Williams has in mind is that if we reject foundationalism, we need not accept the second premise of such arguments, which says that one does not know, say, that one is mistakenly dreaming that p. I shall discuss the status of this premise in Chapter 3. The present point is merely that these simple schematic arguments are not in themselves committed to any overarching philosophical accounts of knowledge or justification.

Another example of an attempt at a global refutation of scepticism is provided by Donald Davidson's account of radical interpretation, which involves a kind of transcendental argument yielding the conclusion that most of our beliefs about the external world must be true.[25] Davidson is a bit vague about the relation between this argument and scepticism, and he cautions that even though we can establish that most of our beliefs must be true, at least some of these true beliefs may fail to qualify as knowledge.[26] Nevertheless, he clearly thinks his argument concerning the possibility of interpretation is of relevance to philosophical scepticism, and other philosophers have taken him to be offering some sort of refutation of it. Klein, for instance, whose characterization of global scep-

25. Donald Davidson, "A Coherence Theory of Knowledge and Truth," in *Truth and Interpretation*, ed. LePore, 307–319.
26. Ibid., 319.

ticism I quoted earlier, takes Davidson to be offering a straightforward refutation of that position, a refutation Klein thinks fails because it appeals to certain things the global sceptic denies we can know to be true.[27] My concern here is not with whether Davidson's argument, or something like Davidson's argument, could be successful, but with whether, even if it is, it provides a satisfactory refutation or diagnosis of the kinds of local sceptical arguments and conclusions I have been discussing.

It seems to me that it does not. Even if such an argument were to yield the conclusion that we know that most of our beliefs about the external world are true, this is perfectly compatible (as Davidson seems to concede) with its not being known that p_1, its not being known that $p_2, \ldots$, and its not being known that p_n, where $p_1 \ldots p_n$ are our external world beliefs. And even if we could establish the more specific conclusion that we know that most of a range of specific propositions must be true, this is still compatible with our failing to know each of those propositions to be true: for example, $K((p_1 \wedge p_2) \vee (p_1 \wedge p_3) \vee (p_2 \wedge p_3))$ is perfectly compatible with each of $\neg Kp_1$, $\neg Kp_2$, $\neg Kp_3$, as well as with their conjunction. And finally, even if we could arrive, via some sort of Davidsonian transcendental argument, at a conclusion incompatible with the conclusions arrived at by the procedure of instantiating the same form of sceptical argument over and over again, this would shed no light at all on where the flaw in the sceptic's arguments or procedure lies—which is something I think a satisfactory refutation or diagnosis of philosophical scepticism has to be able to tell us.

27. Klein, "Radical Interpretation."

CHAPTER TWO

Knowledge and Possibility

In Chapter 1 I raised the question whether there might be, in addition to the sceptical arguments presented there, additional arguments "from possibility," in which claims to know a proposition to be true are undermined not by a failure to *know* that a certain proposition (e.g., one involving some sceptical hypothesis) is false but rather by the epistemic *possibility* that this proposition is true. These epistemic possibilities seem prima facie impersonal and might be thought to inhere, say, in the nature of empirical propositions (as many positivists held), or at least to be characterizable independently of knowledge claims, and thus available to be called on to undermine or rebut claims to know various things. I suggested there that a proper understanding of the relationship between knowledge and possibility would show that these seemingly additional sceptical arguments were not really additional arguments at all, but merely reworded versions of the arguments already presented. This is because, I claimed, the concepts of knowledge and possibility are *duals* of each other: for something to be possible is for it not to be known not to be so, and for something to be known is for it not to be possible that it is not so. But since possibility seems on the surface like an impersonal notion, whereas the basic concept of knowledge seems to be that of individual propositional knowledge, this claim may have seemed implausible. In this chapter I want to look at the concepts of possibility and knowledge before proceeding with our examination of scepticism.

I should say something about the relation between the contents of this chapter (and of Chapter 4) and the account of scepticism that is this book's primary concern. The treatment of scepticism I am trying to develop, which concerns the relation between particular sceptical arguments and the principles of inference that govern them, is to an extent independent of any particular account or analysis of knowledge one might embrace. Yet there are ways of thinking about knowledge which cohere well with, and tend to support, the treatment of scepticism offered here, and which moreover I find independently attractive. In this chapter and in Chapter 4 I want to sketch some of these ways of thinking about knowledge and at least render them plausible, though I shall not try to develop them in much detail (indeed, part of what I want to suggest is that the concept of knowledge is not amenable to certain traditional detailed forms of analysis).

The strategy of this chapter is this: I shall begin by briefly tracing the evolution of our understanding of the notion of epistemic possibility and then look at accounts of that notion offered by several philosophers, accounts that by and large I accept. But these accounts explain epistemic possibility in terms of individual propositional knowledge, which is thus made to seem basic. I shall then turn to the concept of knowledge itself, and argue that what lies at its heart is not the notion of individual knowledge but rather a more impersonal notion of knowledge, and that the former is to be understood in terms of the latter. It is knowledge in this impersonal sense and epistemic possibility that are duals, with neither more basic or fundamental than the other, and neither understandable or explicable independently of the other. I shall then explore some of the features of this concept of knowledge, including its social dimensions.

1. The Evolution of Epistemic Possibility

The course of our understanding of the notion of epistemic possibility has been marked by shifts in the relation it has been taken to bear to the notions of necessity and knowledge. In the first half of the last century a certain form of argument was deployed by a number of philosophers, including C. I. Lewis, Carnap, and Ayer, in an effort to establish that no empirical proposition could ever be known with certainty to be true. This is a claim that I would regard as a strongly sceptical one; yet at the time it was not usually so regarded. Rather, a lack of certainty was taken to be characteristic of empirical knowledge, and the possibility of being falsified taken to be inherent in the notion of an empirical proposition. The argument alleged that any empirical proposition has an infinite number of observational consequences, all of which would have to be verified to occur in order for the proposition to be established with certainty; but that some of these consequences *may* fail to occur—that is, it is always *possi-*

ble that some of them will fail to occur. Hence the proposition cannot be known with absolute certainty to be true.

This argument was subjected to detailed scrutiny by Norman Malcolm in "The Verification Argument," a scrutiny that revealed it to involve a conflation of (what we would now call) logical and epistemic possibility.[1] Malcolm pointed out an ambiguity in the sense of 'may' or 'possible' as it occurs in the argument. He distinguished five senses of the claim that it is possible that the proposition's observational consequences will fail to occur, in two of which it is true: that the statement that the proposition's consequences will fail to occur is not self-contradictory, and that no statement expressing these consequences is entailed by the grounds for holding the proposition to be true. These are notions related to what we would call logical possibility. But for the argument to go through the claim would have to be possible in one of three other senses, which are epistemic in character: that there is some reason to think that the consequences will not occur, that there is no reason to think that they will, or that the grounds for holding that they will occur are not absolutely conclusive. And, Malcolm argued, proponents of the argument had failed to establish that the claim is true in any of these epistemic senses.

G. E. Moore, in entries in his *Commonplace Book, 1919–1953* dating from the early 1940s, had also distinguished what he called epistemic possibility from what he called logical and causal possibility.[2] The latter two tend to be expressed by 'might,' and in the subjunctive mode, as in 'I might have been blind now,' 'It's possible that I should have been blind now,' whereas the former is expressed by 'may,' and in the indicative mode, as in 'Hitler may be dead,' 'It's possible that Hitler is now dead.' Moore equated the epistemic possibility that p with its not being certain that not-p, and noted that the claim, say, that it is epistemically possible that Hitler is now dead is contradicted by the claim that I know that he is not dead.

Ian Hacking, in his article "Possibility," also distinguished epistemic possibility, which he called *L-possibility,* from what he called *M-possibility,* corresponding to what is commonly called logical or metaphysical possibility.[3] He offered an account of the former, to which I shall turn shortly,

1. Norman Malcolm, "The Verification Argument," in *Knowledge and Certainty* (Englewood Cliffs, N.J.: Prentice-Hall, 1963).

2. G. E. Moore, *Commonplace Book, 1919–1953,* ed. Casimir Lewy (London: George Allen & Unwin, 1962), 184–188.

3. Ian Hacking, "Possibility," *Philosophical Review* 76 (1967), 143–168. The distinction between logical and metaphysical possibility need not concern us here.

and argued that it subsumed Malcolm's three senses of epistemic possibility. But although he distinguished L- from M-possibility, he maintained that if something is L-, or epistemically, possible, it must also be M-, or logically, possible. This was called into question by several examples of Rogers Albritton's, cited by Saul Kripke and Hilary Putnam.[4] Albritton argued that it could be held to be epistemically possible for lemons to turn out not to be fruits, or for pencils to turn out to be a peculiar kind of organism—that is, that it is possible that these things should be discovered to be so—even though, assuming that lemons are in fact fruits and that pencils are in fact artifacts and not organisms, it could be held to be necessarily true that lemons are fruits and that pencils are artifacts, and that it is metaphysically impossible that lemons should not have been fruits or that pencils should have been organisms.

Many of the various modalities were untangled in Kripke's *Naming and Necessity*, in which epistemic and metaphysical possibility are treated as completely distinct. For instance, given that Goldbach's conjecture that every even number is the sum of two primes is both unrefuted and unproven, it is epistemically possible that it is true and epistemically possible that it is false. Yet since it is a mathematical proposition, it is, if true, necessarily true, and if false, necessarily false. So either it is not metaphysically possible for Goldbach's conjecture to be true or it is not metaphysically possible for it to be false. Epistemic possibility neither implies nor is implied by logical or metaphysical possibility. But what is it for a proposition to be epistemically possible?

2. Some Accounts of Epistemic Possibility

Since, as Moore noted, the assertion that it is epistemically possible that p is contradicted by my assertion that I know that not-p, it might be held that for p to be epistemically possible is simply for no one to know that not-p, and for it not to be epistemically possible that p is simply for someone to know that not-p. Hacking argued that this proposal is inadequate by way of the following example.[5] A salvage crew is searching for a long-sunken ship, using an old log. The mate of the salvage ship makes some mistaken calculations based on the log and announces that the ship may

4. Saul Kripke, *Naming and Necessity* (Cambridge, Mass.: Harvard University Press, 1980), 23; Hilary Putnam, "The Meaning of 'Meaning'," in *Mind, Language, and Reality: Philosophical Papers, Volume 2* (Cambridge: Cambridge University Press, 1975), 242–243.
5. Hacking, "Possibility," 148.

be in a certain bay—that it is possible that the ship is in that bay. No one knows that it is not in the bay, yet when the log is reexamined and the calculations done correctly, it turns out that the ship could not have gone down there. Hacking maintained that the mate said something false when he said that it was possible that the ship was in the bay. It *seemed* possible to the crew that the ship was there, but a reassessment of the data shows that not to have been a possibility after all.

On the basis of this example Hacking proposed the following working hypothesis concerning epistemic possibility:

> A state of affairs is epistemically possible if it is not known not to obtain, and no practicable investigations would establish that it does not obtain.[6]

Though the mate's careless calculations failed to establish that the ship was not in the bay, it was certainly feasible or practicable for him to have performed those calculations more carefully and to have thereby established that the ship was not there. Hence it was not possible that the ship was there.

What is the force of "practicable investigations" in Hacking's proposal? He notes that it does not mean any *conceivable* investigations, but beyond that does not say. Shortly we will see the need to incorporate a reference to some relevant community in an account of epistemic possibility, and I take it that to say that investigations are "practicable" is to say that there are people in the relevant community who have the qualifications, resources, and opportunities to carry them out, and could carry them out if they chose to do so. Not only is this itself a modal notion, it is also an inherently underdetermined one (I shall say more about underdetermination and epistemic concepts in Chapter 4). I think it points to one of a number of social dimensions to the epistemic notions of possibility and knowledge: investigations, I would suggest, count as practicable if people in the relevant community, if apprised of the qualifications, resources, and opportunities of at least some people in the community, would *agree* by and large that they could be carried out if those people chose to do so. As for "investigations," these of course need not be the kinds of elaborate procedures the word suggests. The "investigations" that establish that there is a cat on the couch or that I have a headache might amount to nothing more than looking at and seeing the cat, or my having the headache and attending to it.

6. Ibid., 149.

Let me also say a word on the force of "establish." To say that an investigative procedure *establishes* that p requires, I take it, that the procedure be *sensitive* to the fact that p. Sensitivity is another modal notion, in this case a counterfactual one. Not only must the procedure lead us to conclude that p if it is in fact the case that p; it also must be that if it had not been the case that p, and circumstances were much as they actually are, then the procedure would have led to the conclusion that not-p. Several philosophers have made proposals as to how this requirement should be spelled out in detail, and I shall not offer any further suggestions here.[7] But I note it now because it will figure in the sequel.

Hacking's proposal says nothing about whose knowledge or lack of it is relevant to an epistemic possibility, or about who must or must not be able to carry out the practicable investigations. Yet it seems clear that a satisfactory account of epistemic possibility must address this issue, perhaps by assigning a role to some kind of community. Suppose my friends know nothing of my whereabouts during spring break and have no idea how to get in touch with me. Recalling my fondness for Paris, they raise the possibility that I've gone there. Surely what they say is not falsified by my own knowledge, or that of my traveling companion, that I'm not in Paris. Or again, the possibility that Goldbach's conjecture is true is surely not refuted by the fact that mathematicians on some inaccessible Twin Earth-like planet have discovered a counterexample to it.

Keith DeRose has proposed an account of epistemic possibility which assigns a role to a relevant community in assessing whether or not something is possible, and which moreover allows for a significant degree of flexibility as to what that community is.[8] His proposal is motivated by a number of examples of the following kind. Suppose a person exhibits some symptoms indicative of cancer, and his doctor decides to run tests that can have one of two outcomes: either cancer is positively ruled out or further tests will have to be run to determine if he actually has cancer. The doctor has received the results of the tests but has yet to inform anyone of their outcome. The patient's wife is asked whether her husband has cancer, and in one scenario she replies that it's possible that he does. At the same time his doctor, knowing the negative outcome of the tests, tells another doctor that it is not possible that the patient has cancer. In

7. See, for instance, Robert Nozick, *Philosophical Explanations* (Cambridge, Mass.: Harvard University Press, 1981), 167–228; Keith DeRose, "Solving the Skeptical Problem," *Philosophical Review* 104 (1995), 1–52; Timothy Williamson, *Knowledge and Its Limits* (Oxford: Oxford University Press, 2000), 147–163.
8. Keith DeRose, "Epistemic Possibilities," *Philosophical Review* 100 (1991), 581–605.

another scenario, though, the patient's wife replies that she doesn't know whether or not it's possible that her husband has cancer: only the doctor, who has seen the test results, knows whether or not there is that possibility.

DeRose argues—plausibly, I think—that all of these responses in the two scenarios, both the wife's and the doctor's, can be taken to be true; and he explains this by arguing that in each case there is a different community of people whose knowledge (or practicable investigations) is relevant to the asserted possibility. When the wife replies in the first scenario that it is possible that her husband has cancer, the relevant community excludes the doctor. But when the doctor asserts that cancer is not a possibility, the relevant community includes him. And in the second scenario, when the wife asserts that she doesn't know whether or not it is possible that her husband has cancer, and that only the doctor knows this, the relevant community does include the doctor. DeRose declines to offer specific proposals for determining the relevant community, beyond saying that it usually (though not always) includes the speaker and her immediate listeners. Instead, he argues that the significance of the examples is that they show both that we must appeal to some relevant community in assessing claims of epistemic possibility and that the relevant community must be taken to be *flexible*, in the sense that it may vary for different assertions or denials of epistemic possibility.[9]

DeRose also maintains that a similar sort of flexibility pertains to the practicable investigations, in Hacking's sense, that are relevant to assessments of possibility. Suppose that the results of the test, which rule out cancer, have been generated by a computer and mailed in an envelope to be received tomorrow. No one, including the doctor, knows what the results are, though it would be practicable to track down the envelope and open it now. Again, in one scenario the patient's wife says that it's possible that her husband has cancer, for he has some of the symptoms; but in a second scenario she says that she doesn't know whether or not it's possible since the results of the test will not be known until tomorrow. In the first scenario the practicable investigation of retrieving and opening the envelope is not being treated as relevant, whereas in the second scenario opening the envelope is being treated as relevant. Since there can be practicable investigations which people in the relevant community are capa-

9. As DeRose notes, the idea of the flexibility of the relevant community and of relevant investigations is also suggested by Paul Teller in "Epistemic Possibility," *Philosophia* 2 (1972), 303–320, and Benjamin Gibbs in "Real Possibility," *American Philosophical Quarterly* 7 (1970), 340–348.

ble of carrying out, yet which are not taken into account in assessing a claim of possibility, it seems that on some occasions the existence of a practicable investigation for establishing that p may be relevant to evaluating an assertion that it is possible that not-p, while on others it may be irrelevant. Combining these two sorts of relevance, DeRose offers the following account of epistemic possibility:

> S's assertion 'It is possible that p' is true if and only if (1) no member of the relevant community knows that p is false, and (2) there is no relevant way that members of the relevant community can come to know that p is false,

where both what count as the relevant community and as relevant ways of knowing are flexible and may vary with the circumstances of assertion.[10]

Let us leave the treatment of epistemic possibility there for now, though we will return to it shortly. But I want to make four observations about DeRose's account. First, clause (1) seems redundant, for if, as (2) requires, there is no relevant way for members of the relevant community to come to know that p is false, then it seems that no one in the community could know that it is. It might be said that someone in the community could have come to know that p is false by employing some practicable but irrelevant method of investigation. Yet if that were so, then there *would* be a relevant way for people in the community to come to know that p is false—namely, by asking that person.

Second, DeRose is proposing truth-conditions for token-assertions of possibility. It would thus be somewhat misleading to say that his account relativizes possibility to communities and methods of investigation. Rather, the token-assertions concern possibility simpliciter, though the truth-conditions of these assertions allude to relevant communities and methods. What these relevant communities and methods are depends on, and may vary with, the circumstances of utterance, and with the proposition the possibility of whose truth is at issue.

Third, DeRose is not offering a traditional kind of analysis of epistemic possibility in terms of necessary and sufficient conditions, for in such traditional analyses the conditions making up the analysis have to be characterizable independently of and conceptually prior to the analysand. But if we look at how his examples work, we see that he does not give any sort of independent characterization of relevant communities and meth-

10. DeRose, "Epistemic Possibilities," 593–594.

ods. Rather, the examples lead us—convincingly, I think— to accept certain verdicts about epistemic possibility; and we then go on to tailor the relevant communities and methods to fit those verdicts. There is nothing wrong with this—indeed, as will become clear eventually, I think that this is a virtue of his account. But while it is important to link epistemic possibility to communities and methods, we should remember that what is conceptually prior in his approach are our verdicts about possibilities rather than the relevance of communities and methods.

Finally, we should note that DeRose's account explains epistemic possibility in terms of individual propositional knowledge. The proposed truth-conditions for possibility have to do with what individuals in the community know or could come to know. Individual propositional knowledge is thus treated as the more basic notion.

3. KNOWLEDGE

Ever since Edmund Gettier refuted the traditional analysis of knowledge as justified true belief, there have been numerous attempts to formulate a satisfactory set of necessary and sufficient conditions for individual propositional knowledge.[11] Given that the history of this endeavor has been a history of counterexamples, one may wonder why so many philosophers have persisted in it. Perhaps the explanation goes something like this: individual propositional knowledge is the basic notion of knowledge and the basic concept of epistemology, and it obviously amounts to more than merely true belief; so given its centrality, it is important to try to explicate it by identifying what in addition to true belief it involves.

There are reasons, though, to doubt the prospects for the success of this endeavor, and to question its motivation. As Timothy Williamson has pointed out, given that true belief is necessary but insufficient for knowledge, it does not follow that there is some additional condition, characterizable independently of knowledge, which along with true belief is sufficient for knowledge.[12] To use his example, being colored is necessary but insufficient for being red; yet there is no additional condition, char-

11. Edmund Gettier, "Is Justified True Belief Knowledge?" *Analysis* 23 (1963), 121–123. For an account of attempts to formulate a satisfactory analysis of individual propositional knowledge, see Robert Shope, *The Analysis of Knowing: A Decade of Research* (Princeton: Princeton University Press, 1983).

12. Timothy Williamson, "Is Knowing a State of Mind?" *Mind* 104 (1995), 533–565, and *Knowledge and Its Limits*, 3.

acterizable independently of being red, which along with being colored is sufficient for being red. Indeed, apart from the philosophically unimportant concepts of bachelorhood and vixenhood, it is hard to find any examples of concepts, let alone philosophically interesting ones, which can be successfully analyzed into necessary and sufficient conditions.

Some broad reasons to doubt that individual propositional knowledge is amenable to such an analysis seem fairly clear. Gettier's counterexamples to the traditional analysis are ones in which someone has a justified belief that is correct only by accident. Externalist accounts that rule out accidentally true beliefs by requiring some sort of appropriately reliable connection between beliefs and the states of affairs they represent seem to marginalize the role of reasons and evidence in knowledge, and thus seem too weak. Internalist accounts that strengthen the justification condition to require the possession of *conclusive* reasons seem to require too much of us, since we are usually not in possession of reasons that, in any literal sense, can be called conclusive. Moreover, it is hard to say just what "conclusive" means here. To have conclusive reasons for the belief that p presumably enables one to rule out the possibility that not-p. But as we have just seen, received accounts of epistemic possibility explicate it in terms of individual propositional knowledge.

Much of the impetus for the attempt to analyze individual propositional knowledge in the traditional way (and one of the reasons why that attempt is unlikely to be successful) comes from the assumption that individual propositional knowledge is the fundamental mode of knowledge. For if it is, there is a strong temptation to try to incorporate all the factors relevant to knowledge into conditions satisfied by individual knowers. But in practice our relations to propositions we know to be true are much more casual than most detailed analyses suggest. If someone knows that p, then the truth of p has been established; but there is often little that is true of that person, considered in isolation from his social setting, that bears on the establishment of p's truth. If someone asks me if I know that a mutual friend of ours has a new car, my affirmative answer is acceptable even though I'd only heard a passing remark to that effect. Or I may know that Fermat's Last Theorem is true simply because I read in a magazine that it had been proven, or because I overheard a conversation in which this was mentioned, even though this way of arriving at a belief in the truth of FLT, considered in isolation, seems wholly insufficient for knowledge. The right way to characterize my epistemic situation is to say that I exist in a context—a social context—in which the information about the truth of FLT is there for the taking, and that I have obtained that information in a way that is recognized to be legitimate. Put another way, a person can know that p if he inhabits a social context, or belongs to a community, in which the knowledge that p is *available,* and he simply avails himself of it. On this way of looking at the matter, the fundamental concept of knowledge is the impersonal concept of the knowledge that p's being available to members of a community. Individual knowledge is then to be understood in terms of a person in that community's availing himself of knowledge in this impersonal sense.[13]

What does it mean to say that the knowledge that p is available? Let me make it clear at the outset that I shall not try to offer a traditional analysis of the notion in terms of necessary and sufficient conditions. I am sure that if one were to attempt such a thing, the same kinds of familiar difficulties and counterexamples would arise that one encounters in attempting to analyze individual propositional knowledge. My purpose is simply to suggest that the impersonal notion of knowledge is more basic than the individual one. But I think it can be understood in terms of some of the notions that came up in our discussion of possibility. To say that the knowledge that p is available is to say that there are relevant practicable ways or methods for people in some relevant community to establish that p. This does not mean that everyone in the community is capable of establishing that p. Andrew Wiles and a few other mathematicians are capable of establishing the truth of FLT, though I and most other people are not; and yet the knowledge of the truth of FLT is available to me. Whether the knowledge that p is available or not depends on whether or not the truth of p can actually be established. Wiles's first proof of FLT was defective, though this was not discovered for some time. The knowledge of the truth of FLT was not then available (though it seemed to be), and had I read a magazine article or overheard a conversation then, I would not have known that FLT was true. When Wiles fixed the proof, the knowledge of the truth of FLT actually became available, and by reading of it in a magazine or overhearing a conversation then, I could come to know of its truth, even though my own relation to the proposition that FLT is true, considered in isolation from my social setting, would have been the same

13. Williamson introduces a notion similar to that of knowledge's being available, that of being in a position to know, in "Cognitive Homelessness," *Journal of Philosophy* 93 (1996), 554–573: "To be in a position to know that P, it is neither necessary to know that P nor sufficient to be physically and psychologically capable of knowing that P. No obstacle must block one's path to knowing that P. If one is in a position to know that P, and has done what one is in a position to do to decide whether P, then one does know that P. The fact is open to one's view, unhidden, even if one does not yet see it" (555).

as my earlier relation. Also, as Hacking's example of the sunken ship suggests, the knowledge that p can be available even though no one in the relevant community has actually established that p or knows that p. A careful examination of the log by the salvage ship's mate would establish that the sunken ship is not in the bay; and so even though the mate has not carried out that examination, the knowledge that the ship is not in the bay is available. This example also indicates that for me to avail myself of that knowledge may require the cooperation of others. If I am not capable of properly examining the log myself, then I cannot avail myself of the knowledge that the ship is not in the bay—by, for instance, asking the mate—until the mate or some other competent person has actually examined the log properly.

What is it for a person to *avail* himself of available knowledge? Assuming for now that knowledge involves belief (an issue to be considered in section 5), availing one's self of the knowledge that p amounts to coming to believe that p in some epistemically *legitimate* way, where legitimacy is ultimately to be understood in social terms. A person has come to know that p in an epistemically legitimate way if his claim to know that p would be accepted by and large by members of the community apprised of how he came by the belief and aware of the availability of the knowledge that p. Reading of the proof of FLT in an ordinary magazine is legitimate in this sense; reading of the details of some celebrity's sex life in one of the research journals at the supermarket checkout station is not. A glance across a field may be a legitimate way of coming to believe that there is a barn there, though perhaps not if one is in the kind of region, so familiar to epistemologists, in which barn facades proliferate. These examples suggest that a legitimate way of coming by a belief should be to some extent sensitive to the fact one believes to obtain. And while this is true, my suggestion is that what is basic is the *acceptance* by people in the community of claims to know things one has come to believe by the way in question. If that way is grossly insensitive, that acceptance may be unlikely; still, it is the acceptance, rather than the sensitivity, that determines the legitimacy of a way of coming by a belief.

Because of this, to say that one knows that p just in case one comes to believe that p in a legitimate way when the knowledge that p is available is not to offer yet another analysis of individual knowledge in terms of necessary and sufficient conditions, since the concept of the legitimacy of a way of coming by a belief cannot be characterized independently of the concept of knowledge. In Chapter 4 I shall extend this treatment of knowledge by rejecting what Williams calls epistemological realism, according to which knowledge claims are true or false independently of whether we accept or reject them, and arguing instead that claims to knowledge are made true by our general acceptance of them.[14] If so, then the legitimacy of a way of coming by a belief depends on whether or not we would accept a claim to knowledge made by someone who acquires a belief in that way—which is to say on whether or not someone who acquires a belief in that way knows what he claims to know. And the same is true of our account of what it is for the knowledge that p to be available—namely, that there be relevant ways for people in the relevant community to establish that p. As I noted of DeRose's account of epistemic possibility, our notions of relevant ways and relevant communities are responsive to our assessments of possibility rather than vice versa. Similarly, our assessments of relevant ways and relevant communities—and of whether p can be established in those ways—are responsive to our assessment of whether the knowledge that p is available. The various epistemic concepts that have been in play here—possibility, individual knowledge, available knowledge, legitimate ways of acquiring beliefs, relevant methods, relevant communities, the establishment of the truth of a proposition—are related in the ways indicated, but ultimately the extensions of those concepts are determined by the claims to knowledge we make and accept in practice. At any rate, that is the view I am trying to develop here and in Chapter 4.[15]

4. Knowledge and Possibility as Duals

We are now in a position to see that the concept of epistemic possibility and the impersonal concept of the knowledge that p's being available are dual notions: it is possible that p just in case the knowledge that not-p is not available; and the knowledge that p is available just in case it is not possible that not-p. Consider DeRose's account of epistemic possibility, which I take to be basically correct: it is possible that p just in case (1) no one knows that not-p and (2) there are no relevant ways that members of the relevant community can come to know that not-p.[16] Given the re-

---

14. Michael Williams, *Unnatural Doubts* (Cambridge: Basil Blackwell, 1991), 87–134.

15. Gilbert Harman also proposes appealing to ordinary judgments about knowledge to characterize subsidiary epistemic concepts. See *Thought* (Princeton: Princeton University Press, 1973), 15–23.

16. DeRose's actual proposal concerns the truth-conditions for token-assertions of possibility, but I have modified it for purposes of the present discussion.

dundancy of (1), this means that it is possible that p just in case there are no relevant ways for members of the relevant community to come to know that not-p, and so to establish that not-p; and if not, then the knowledge that not-p is not available. Conversely, if the knowledge that not-p is not available, then there are no relevant ways for members of the relevant community to establish that p, and thereby come to know that p; and if not, then it is possible that p. Similar reasoning shows that the knowledge that p is available just in case it is not possible that not-p. Hence the concepts of available knowledge and epistemic possibility are duals.

Given this, we cannot simply appeal to epistemic possibilities to undermine claims to knowledge, as sceptical arguments from possibility would have us do. The verification argument that Malcolm so effectively dismantled sought to establish the impossibility of knowing any empirical proposition with certainty by alleging a possibility of falsification inherent in the very concept of an empirical proposition; but that argument, as Malcolm showed, was fallacious. We may be tempted, though, by a similar fallacy. Faced with a claim to know that p, or a claim that the knowledge that p is available, we may be tempted to rebut it by citing the apparent fact that on reflection we realize that there is always the possibility of being mistaken in thinking that p. Now this may indeed be so—we will consider sceptical claims regarding outré possibilities in the next chapter. But the present point is that to try to rebut a claim to know that p by citing the possibility that not-p is not to provide any sort of reason or argument against the knowledge claim; it is simply to respond to one epistemic claim by denying it, by asserting a proposition that is tantamount to its negation.

Of course, it might *seem* to someone that a possibility of mistake exists when it does not. Given the casual relation I have suggested may obtain between a person and a proposition of the knowledge of whose truth he has availed himself, I may readily concede that FLT may turn out to be false after all, given my almost total ignorance of the particulars of its proof. But on the present view, my concession would be mistaken: there is no such possibility.

In Chapter 4 I shall argue that the extension of the concept of knowledge—that is, the propositions that count as known—is determined by our epistemic practices, by the knowledge claims we in fact accept. This allows that our practices *could* have been somewhat different than they are—we could have been more permissive about what we accept as known, or we could have been more demanding (whether we could have been demanding enough to accept the conclusions of sceptical arguments is unclear to me, though I have no argument that we could not have been).

Suppose it is objected that the standards we have, or some even more permissive standards we might have employed, are too loose, in that they lead us to accept claims to know things that might possibly be false. If knowledge and possibility are duals, as I have argued, there is no standpoint from which to launch this objection, for the extension of the concept of epistemic possibility is determined by exactly the same practices and standards to which we would be objecting.

All this may seem to make a refutation of scepticism relatively easy, by severely restricting the range of possibilities the sceptic can legitimately invoke. In Chapters 3 and 5 I shall argue that this is far from the case.

5. KNOWLEDGE AND MENTAL STATES

A qualm one might have about treating the impersonal notion of the availability of knowledge, rather than personal knowledge, as fundamental is that it may seem to fail to do justice to the idea that knowledge is a condition persons can be in or aspire to be in. We tend to think of knowledge as something that people, in the pursuit of inquiry, strive to attain; and so the pursuit of knowledge often seems to figure in an explanation of a person's behavior. Moreover, the *possession* of knowledge may also be thought to explain individual conduct: my stubborn persistence in looking for a missing sock in my dresser drawer may seem to become explicable if I am taken to know, rather than merely believe, that the sock is in the drawer.[17] But if individual knowledge is merely a matter of a person's being casually, albeit legitimately, related to the situation of knowledge's being available, it may seem an insufficiently robust notion to play the explanatory roles some take it to play.

H. A. Pritchard maintained that personal knowledge was a genuine mental state, a state disjoint from the mental state of belief: if you know that p, then you do *not* (merely) believe that p.[18] Most philosophers were unpersuaded by this, for at least two reasons: first, belief is a component in the traditional analysis of knowledge as justified true belief; and second, it seemed obvious that one can be in the same state internally, and hence mentally, whether p is true or not.

17. See Williamson, *Knowledge and Its Limits*, 62. Mark Kaplan, though, has argued that examples like this can be handled by using the Bayesian notion of a *resilient* belief: "Who Cares What You Know?" *Philosophical Quarterly* 53 (2003), 105–116.

18. H. A. Pritchard, *Knowledge and Perception* (Oxford: Oxford University Press, 1950), 86.

Williamson has recently revived the idea that a person's knowing that p is a genuine state of mind, by arguing against both of these reasons for rejecting Pritchard's proposal.[19] First, he has argued against the idea that individual knowledge is amenable to an analysis into necessary and sufficient conditions, one of which is belief; and as we have seen, this rejection of the analyzability of knowledge is congenial to the view of knowledge I am trying to develop here. Second, he has argued that if we adopt an externalist conception of mental states, as Tyler Burge and many other philosophers have urged, then it does not follow from the fact that one can be in the same internal condition whether or not p is true that one would be in the same mental state whether or not p is true.[20] Williamson has proposed that knowledge be regarded as a factive mental state. A mental state is factive if it has propositional content, and one is in the state only if the proposition expressing that content is true: remembering that p and seeing that p are thus factive mental states. His proposal is that knowledge is simply the most general factive mental state, subsuming, for instance, remembering that and seeing that. He has defended this proposal against a variety of objections, and argued that it allows us to do justice to the role knowledge seems to play in the explanation of individual conduct.

I do not mean to endorse Williamson's proposal, but I do want to suggest that not only is it compatible with the view of knowledge I have suggested here, but the present view of knowledge actually seems to me to enhance it. On his view, someone is in the state of mind of knowing that p only if some appropriate external condition is satisfied. He does not actually say what the external condition is supposed to be, beyond saying that it involves p's being true. But since he argues persuasively that we can view knowledge as a mental state, while rejecting the idea that believing truly is a mental state, the appropriate external condition presumably involves more than just p's being true.[21] I would suggest that the appropriate external condition is that the knowledge that p be available. Thus to be in the mental state of knowing that p is to have legitimately come by a belief that p in a relevant community in which there are relevant ways of establishing that p. This is not quite to endorse Williamson's view of knowledge as a distinctive mental state, though I

19. Williamson, "Is Knowing a State of Mind?" and *Knowledge and Its Limits*, 21–48.

20. Tyler Burge, "Individualism and the Mental," *Midwest Studies in Philosophy* 4 (1979), 73–121.

21. Williamson, "Is Knowing a State of Mind?" 538–540, and *Knowledge and Its Limits*, 27–30.

do find the view attractive in many respects. Rather, the point is to assuage the qualms of those who feel that the present account of knowledge depersonalizes it too much and leaves it incapable of playing the kind of explanatory roles we take it to play, by noting that it fits in nicely with a view of individual knowledge as a robust state of mind.

Williamson leaves open the question whether someone in the mental state of knowing that p is also in the mental state of believing that p. He argues that his account of knowledge is compatible with either a positive or negative answer to the question, though his discussion suggests that he inclines toward the latter. On the treatment of knowledge I have suggested here belief *is* a component of knowledge, since to know that p involves coming to believe that p in a legitimate way. Let me indicate why I think that we should continue to hold that knowing involves believing.

Much depends on how we think of belief. If belief were a mental state characterized primarily by its causal role in the production of behavior, and if knowledge were also taken to be a mental state that plays a role in the production and explanation of behavior, there might indeed be a real question whether being in the latter state involves being in the former: they might very well be disjoint states. But this does not seem to me to be the best way to think of belief.[22] Belief should be thought of as the most general proattitude toward a proposition, and characterized as the condition of someone who takes the position that p, is of a mind that p, or is prepared to assert that p; and thought of in this way, knowing that p *does* involve believing that p, since to know that p typically involves being prepared to assert that p (indeed, for Williamson, to assert that p one is required to know that p).[23]

Moreover, consider a person who knows that p, and an assessment made of this person by someone who does not know that p or take herself to know that p (and may even have no position on the question whether or not p). She hears the person who knows that p assert that p, and on the basis of this assertion ascribes to him the belief that p; moreover, she could not, unless she took herself to know that p, attribute to him the knowledge that p. If knowledge and belief are disjoint mental states, then not only must we say that her assessment of the knower is in-

22. One reason is that it opens the door to eliminativism, for it may turn out that no state playing a causal role in the production of behavior has the properties of belief.
23. Williamson, "Knowing and Asserting," *Philosophical Review* 105 (1996), 489–523, and *Knowledge and Its Limits*, 238–269. I am leaving aside the kinds of cases Colin Radford considers in "Knowledge—By Examples," *Analysis* 27 (1966), 1–11, in which someone knows something he is apparently unprepared to assert.

correct; we must also say that she cannot in principle make a correct assessment of his actual mental state. (Notice that this indicates a peculiarity of the view that knowledge is a mental state: unlike other mental states, it can be attributed to a person only by someone who takes herself to be in the same mental state. Whether or not this peculiarity is objectionable is unclear to me.) I am sympathetic to a Davidson-like view of belief and other intentional states, on which people are in them by virtue of their being interpreted by others to be in them.[24] If one shares this sympathy, one should be reluctant to adopt a view of knowledge that requires us to reject the non-knower's assessment of the knower as simply incorrect.

6. Social Dimensions of Knowledge

There are a number of respects in which the concept of knowledge (and possibility) is socially determined. For the knowledge that p to be available depends on the existence of relevant practicable ways for people in a relevant community to establish that p. The notion of a relevant community is obviously a social one, and what count as "practicable" and "relevant" methods also depend on the people's assessments, as does whether or not p can be "established." And for an individual to know that p is for him to have come by a belief that p in a legitimate way in the context of the knowledge that p's being available; but what counts as a "legitimate" way of coming by a belief depends on people's assessments of whether someone coming by a belief in that way qualifies as knowing.

I shall develop this conception of knowledge further in Chapter 4, but now I want to raise the question whether knowledge is an *inherently* social concept, and argue that it should be answered affirmatively. Some things that are a matter of social convention are not inherently so: forms of clothing, for example, are largely a matter of social convention, but that does not mean that people could not be said to be clothed in the absence of social conventions concerning attire. So even if what count as legitimate, relevant, and practicable methods, and so on, depend on people's epistemic assessments, we can still ask whether the concept of knowledge might nevertheless be applicable to individuals considered in isolation from any social setting. And it seems to me that the answer to this is no.

We can mount an argument for this conclusion along the lines of

24. See, for example, "Radical Interpretation" and "Thought and Talk," in *Inquiries into Truth and Interpretation* (Oxford: Oxford University Press, 1984).

Wittgenstein's private language argument, or as I prefer to call it, his argument against a solitary speaker. I have discussed this argument in detail elsewhere, and shall only sketch here how I take it to go.[25] The question is whether or not there could be a person who uses a language that could not, even in principle, be understood by others, and consequently whose use of the language is not subject to assessment by others. If so, there must be a distinction between, say, his correctly asserting that p and its merely *seeming* (to him) that his assertion that p is correct.[26] If there *is* such a distinction, then it must be possible to draw it—it must be possible for someone to be in a position to *say* that an assertion of his that p only seems correct but is not in fact so (that someone can be in a position to say this does not entail that what he says is *true*—thus the argument is not verificationist in character). But no one other than him can make such an assessment, since his use of the language is not subject to assessment by others. And *he* cannot make such an assessment of himself, since the circumstances that license his assertion that p coincide with those that license the assertion that it seems (to him) that p. So no one can be in a position to draw the distinction between an assertion of his being correct and its merely seeming to be so.

That the conditions that license the assertion that p coincide with those that license the assertion that it seems that p is part of a general diagnosis I have proposed elsewhere of what is called Moore's paradox, which concerns the unassertibility of utterances like 'It's raining, but I don't believe it,' 'I believe that p, but not-p,' 'It seems to me that p, but not-p,' "P, but I don't know that p,' and many others.[27] The general diagnosis maintains that the assertibility-conditions of propositions E(p) involving the contexts involved in Moore's paradox—'I believe that p,' 'It seems to me that p,' 'I know that p,' and so on—coincide with the assertibility-conditions of p itself, even though the truth-conditions of these propositions differ from those of p.[28]

25. See my *The Continuity of Wittgenstein's Thought* (Ithaca: Cornell University Press, 1996), 139–144.
26. 'Correct' here need not mean 'true,' but rather something like 'in accordance with the rules of usage governing p.'
27. See my "A Note on Moore's Paradox," *Philosophical Studies* 34 (1978), 303–310, and *Continuity of Wittgenstein's Thought*, 144–151.
28. Strictly, the claim is that the assertibility-conditions of p are a subset of those of E(p), which allows for the assertibility of 'I believe that p, but I don't know it.' This approach to Moore's paradox was suggested by Wittgenstein in section x of Part II of *Philosophical Investigations*, 3d ed., trans. G. E. M. Anscombe (New York: Macmillan, 1968), where he remarks that 'I believe that this is the case' has the same use as 'This is the case.'

Now let us suppose—what must be impossible if the argument against a solitary speaker is correct—that there is an individual able to make assertions and claims and have beliefs but whose assertions and beliefs are not subject to epistemic assessment by others. Could the concept of knowledge still apply to this person? That is, could it be true that some of his beliefs qualified as knowledge while others did not? For him to qualify as, say, knowing that p, there must be a distinction between his knowing that p and his merely believing truly that p, for such a distinction is inherent in the concept of knowledge. But for there to *be* such a distinction, it must be possible to draw it, that is, to *say* (not necessarily truly) that he does not know that p but merely believes truly that p. But since he is not subject to assessment by others, no one other than himself can be in a position to say this. And since the assertibility-conditions for 'I know that p' and 'It is true that p' and 'I truly believe that p' coincide, *he* can never be in a position to distinguish between his knowing that p and his merely believing truly that p. But if this distinction cannot be drawn, the concept of knowledge is not applicable to him.

This argument—call it the argument against a solitary knower—should not be taken to show that there can never be a case in which the relevant community to whose members the knowledge that p is available (or not available) is a community of one. As we shall see shortly, for some propositions this is indeed the case. But first, this is not the case for *all* propositions: typically, when knowledge is available (or not available) to me, it is also available (or not) to others in a community to which I belong. And second, even when the relevant community consists of myself alone, others *are* able to make the assessment that, say, I do not know the proposition in question to be true (even though I truly believe it). Rather, the argument is intended to show that the concept of knowledge is inherently social in that it can apply to an individual only if that application is subject to the assessment of others.

7. Some Vagaries of the First Person

The assessment of claims of knowledge and possibility depends on what can be established by members of some relevant community. When the claim concerns the truth of an "impersonal" proposition like the truth of FLT, the relevant community basically consists of everyone in a position to reach an informed opinion on the matter in a relevant way. But when the proposition concerns a person—a person, for instance, belonging to the community relevant to epistemic claims about FLT—the question of the relevant community becomes more complicated. As I noted earlier, my knowledge of my own whereabouts may not be relevant to assertions made by others that there is a possibility that I am presently in Paris. I may know that I am not, but if it is not practicable to track me down, then my knowledge does not falsify those assertions. And my traveling companion also presumably knows that I am not in Paris, yet she may also be excluded from the community relevant to the assessment of those claims by others. At what point does the community centered on me overlap or merge with the one relevant to the assessment of others' assertions of possibility concerning my present whereabouts? It is hard to give a general answer since it depends on what, given the facts of the case, it is practicable for them to find out. But the point is simply that even if the peculiarities of the circumstances exclude me and my immediate circle from the community relevant to the assessment of assertions concerning my present whereabouts, we may all nevertheless belong to the community relevant to assessments of assertions concerning FLT.

The point of course applies to an individual's knowledge of his own mental states, but it is not confined to knowledge of mental states, and I am not suggesting that claims of knowledge and possibility concerning an individual's mental states should be treated differently from other claims. I may raise the possibility that a colleague of mine is at the moment very angry about something, not knowing myself that he is not. But if it would be practicable for me to walk down the hall and witness for myself his sunny disposition, then that possibility is ruled out. But the same is true about the possibility that he is not in his office at the moment: if it is practicable for me to look and see that he is, then that possibility is similarly ruled out. (In these cases his own knowledge of his present mental condition and whereabouts *is* relevant to an assessment of the possibilities I raise.)

The Paris example suggests that when the proposition whose epistemic status is being assessed concerns an individual, it is often the case that knowledge is available to that person which is not available to others, so that he is to be excluded from the relevant community to which they belong. But it can work the other way as well: knowledge concerning an individual can be available to others which is *not* available to the individual himself (so that, again, he is excluded from the relevant community to which they belong). Cases like this arise in particular in the consideration of scepticism.

In the next chapter we will consider responses to scepticism that try to deny the truth of one or more of the premises of sceptical arguments. In dreaming-type arguments, the crucial premise is that I do not know, say, that I am not a brain in a vat having subjective experiences and thoughts that lead me to mistakenly believe that I am sitting at my desk. To anticipate a bit, I will argue in the next chapter that responses to scepticism that deny the truth of this premise are unsatisfactory. Assume for the sake of argument that this is correct, and that I do not now know that I am not a brain in a vat (etc.). The reason I do not know it is that the knowledge that I am not is not available to me, for the sceptical hypothesis was formulated specifically to make this knowledge unavailable to me. Nevertheless, I want to suggest, the knowledge that I, JK, am not a deluded brain in a vat may be readily available to others. Anyone who drops by my office, observes my present circumstances, and perhaps engages me in conversation knows perfectly well that I am not a brain in a vat. Noting the topic I'm engaged in writing about, they may even offer their assurances that I am not. Yet these assurances would not, I want to maintain, endow me with the knowledge that I am not now a brain in a vat (for the sceptical hypothesis was specifically constructed so that they would not). But if my visitor were to offer me similar assurances about the truth of FLT, I would, it seems to me, come to know that FLT is true.

What this means is that when I am assessing claims of knowledge or possibility concerning a sceptical hypothesis about myself, the relevant community is a community of one, a community limited to me alone. Others may correctly arrive at a different assessment, but that is irrelevant to the correctness of my own assessment. DeRose makes a similar observation about Descartes' *Meditations* when he writes that "readers are being invited only to listen in on his meditations, and . . . the relevant community is limited to Descartes himself."[29] Although he does not elaborate, to say that it is a matter of what Descartes is inviting his readers to do seems to suggest that this is a consequence of Descartes' intentions in writing the *Meditations.* By contrast, my suggestion is that to the extent that Descartes is concerned with sceptical possibilities, the limitation of the relevant community to one consisting of Descartes alone is inherent in the very subject matter of his meditations.

8. Sceptical Arguments Revisited

The sceptical arguments surveyed in Chapter 1 were formulated in terms of personal knowledge: for instance, if one knows that one has

29. DeRose, "Epistemic Possibilities," 595.

teeth, then one must know that one is not a brain in a vat (etc.); but one does not know the latter; therefore, one does not know that one has teeth. These arguments were seen to involve what I called the transmission principle, also formulated there in terms of personal knowledge: if one knows that p_1, knows that p_2, ..., knows that p_n, and if one knows that these imply q, then one also knows that q. The arguments and principle were formulated using a propositional operator Kp, glossed as expressing personal knowledge, even though it was not explicitly indexed to a person.

Given the treatment of knowledge (and possibility) offered in this chapter, we can now see that sceptical arguments and the transmission principle can be reformulated in terms of the impersonal notion of the knowledge that p's being available. Thus if the knowledge that I have teeth is available (to me), then the knowledge that I am not a brain in a vat must also be available (to me); but the latter knowledge is not available (to me), so neither is the former. And if the knowledge that p_1 is available, the knowledge that p_2 is available, and so on, and if the knowledge that these imply q is available, then so is the knowledge that q. (As the parenthetical qualifiers "to me" indicate, individuals still play a crucial role in these versions of the arguments, but now it is as members of some relevant community.) The propositional operator Kp would now be glossed as expressing the availability of the knowledge that p.

These versions of our sceptical arguments formulated in terms of the notion of knowledge's being available are in some ways preferable. On the present treatment of knowledge, there are two ways that an individual can fail to know something: either the knowledge is not available to him, or he has failed to avail himself of it by coming by the belief in question in a legitimate way. It seems clear that sceptical arguments seek to establish the former sort of failure to know. The sceptic is not maintaining that I do not know that I do not, say, have teeth merely because I have failed to undertake a procedure I was in a position to undertake, or followed a route to belief that was open to me. Rather, the claim is that I do not know this because, given my inability to rule out some appropriate sceptical hypothesis, I *cannot* know this: that knowledge is simply not available to me. Also, the reformulated versions make clear that there is not an additional sceptical argument from possibility, and more broadly, that there is no independently characterizable notion of epistemic possibility which can be appealed to in order to support or rebut sceptical (and other) claims concerning the extent of knowledge.

It might be thought though that reformulated in terms of the availability of knowledge, sceptical arguments involve a fallacy of equivocation. Claims about the availability of knowledge appeal to a relevant community, and the community relevant to the knowledge whose availability is being challenged—for instance, that FLT is true, or that there is a cat on the couch—may differ from the community relevant to the availability of the knowledge that some appropriate sceptical hypothesis is false (which, as I just argued, is a community of one). So it may appear that the expression 'the knowledge that p is available' has a different meaning in the premise of the argument than it has in the conclusion.

In the next two chapters we shall consider the idea that the meaning of words like 'knowledge' and 'know' is subject to variation. But the present case is not one in which this is happening. The community relevant to the availability of the knowledge that a particular proposition is true depends on the proposition, and varies with the proposition in question. But this does not mean that the meaning of the epistemic expression varies too. Claims about the availability of knowledge or about epistemic possibilities also appeal to relevant ways or methods of establishing the truth of a proposition, and these relevant ways or methods will vary depending on the proposition in question. The methods relevant to establishing the truth of FLT differ from those relevant to establishing that Hacking's ship did not go down in the bay. But this does not mean that one is using words in different senses when one says that it is possible neither that FLT is false nor that the ship is in the bay, or when one says that the knowledge that FLT is true and the knowledge that the ship is not in the bay are both available. We will return to the question of the meaning of epistemic terms later.

Having said all this, it must be conceded that talk about whether or not the knowledge that p is available, and so on, is something of a mouthful, and it is certainly clearer and more economical to talk simply about whether or not I know that p. So I shall usually frame the discussion of sceptical arguments in terms of personal knowledge, unless the more cumbersome formulations are actually to the point. Let us return now to an examination of those arguments.

The Status of the Sceptic's Premises

In Chapter 1 I inventoried a number of sceptical arguments, bringing out the role played in them by a principle of inference called the transmission principle, according to which knowledge is transmitted from propositions known to be true to propositions known to be consequences of those propositions. A straightforward refutation of sceptical arguments would take one of two forms: establishing that one or more of their premises are false, or establishing that the inferences they involve—inferences governed by the transmission principle—are invalid. In this chapter I want to consider responses to sceptical arguments of the first sort, and in Chapter 5 I will take up the question of the validity of the transmission principle.

The arguments surveyed in Chapter 1 included dreaming-type arguments, which are by far the best-known and most important sceptical arguments, as well as what I called the argument from fallibility and an argument attributed to Kripke. There is little point in considering the latter two arguments in this chapter, as their premises seem beyond reproach. The crucial premise of the argument from fallibility is that there are bound to be some falsehoods among the propositions that have survived one's strictest epistemic scrutiny. Although there may be rare instances in which this is false, a satisfactory rebuttal of the sceptic's arguments surely should not have to rest on the supposition of such epistemic good fortune. In the Kripkean argument the crucial (second) premise is that if one knows a proposition to be true, then one knows that any apparent evidence against it is misleading evidence for something false. This claim may indeed be subject to challenge; but as we saw in Chapter 1, to challenge it is to challenge the validity of the transmission principle, since it is by that principle that it is inferred from the obviously true first premise that if a proposition is true, then any apparent evidence against it is evidence for something false.

We shall concentrate, then, on the crucial premise of dreaming-type arguments: that I do not know to be false a sceptical hypothesis to the effect that the proposition I am considering, which common sense says I know to be true, is actually false, though it *seems* to be true because I am having a vivid dream to that effect, or because I am at the mercy of some deceitful demon controlling my thoughts and experiences, or because I am a brain in a vat being manipulated by alien scientists, or for some other far-fetched though seemingly logically possible reason along those lines. I shall first summarize the basic case in favor of this premise and then consider briefly three strategies for denying it: a dismissal of it out of hand, the strategy adopted by G. E. Moore; an argument some philosophers have sought to extract from Wittgenstein's discussion of Moore in *On Certainty;* and arguments against it based on an inference to the best explanation. Then I shall consider at somewhat greater length the subtlest strategy for dealing with the premise, a view known as *contextualism,* which holds that the entertainment of the sceptic's argument creates a "context" in which both premises and conclusion are true, but that in ordinary, everyday contexts both premises and conclusion are false. Contextualism thus attempts to account for the allure of dreaming-type arguments while vindicating common-sense claims to knowledge. But I shall argue that none of these strategies affords a satisfactory rebuttal of the sceptic's arguments.

1. The Seductiveness of Sceptical Hypotheses

There is a certain dialectic to our engagement with sceptical arguments which it is important to keep in mind. As we see in Descartes' First Meditation, our attention is first drawn to some belief that seems paradigmatic of those that common sense takes it as obvious we know to be true: that I am sitting at a desk, that I have teeth, and so on. A scenario or hypothesis is then introduced which at first seems utterly unrelated to the belief under consideration, which common sense has almost certainly *not* previously considered or taken a position on, and which at first seems outlandish or even of dubious intelligibility: for instance, that one is a bodiless and toothless brain in a vat whose experiences and thoughts are being inculcated by alien scientists intent on engendering the illusion that one is a freshman student in an introductory philosophy course at a large state university. But as the scenario or hypothesis is developed and elaborated, not only does it come to seem intelligible in a perverse way—after all, it is capable of sustaining a feature-length movie like *The Matrix*—but one is led, on reflection, to the acknowledgment that a claim to know the hypothesis to be false seems indefensible (Descartes: "When I consider these matters carefully, I realise so clearly that there are no conclusive indications by which waking life can be distinguished from sleep that I am quite astonished")[1]. And finally, as its relation to the original commonsense belief emerges, one comes to the apparent realization that since one cannot rule out this hypothesis and thereby come to know it to be false, the presumption that one knows, say, that one has teeth has been undermined.

That sceptical hypotheses are initially *surprising* is part of what makes any claim to know them to be false seem indefensible (Descartes: "I am quite astonished"). For it seems a general rule, though not an exceptionless one, that if we know something, there must be some way in which we have *come* to know it, or some answer to the question *how* we know it. And of course the whole point of sceptical hypotheses is that they seem to foreclose any such answer. Since we have not previously considered them, any answer to the question how we know them to be false is not going to lie close at hand. And as we begin to consider them, we come to realize that any investigation or procedure we might undertake in an attempt to refute them would not constitute a satisfactory way of coming to know them to be false, since they are specifically formulated to be compatible with an apparently positive outcome to any practicable such investigation or procedure, which would thus fail to be sensitive to the truth or falsity of the hypotheses.[2] Of course there are some beliefs that we can know to be true without there being a substantive answer to the question *how* we know them—for instance, I know that I am thinking about scepticism, but the only "answer" to the question how I know this is that I am. And there are things that we know to be true without being able to *say* how we know them. I know that Paris is the capital of France, and am confident that there is some way, or many ways, in which I came to know this, but I am quite unable to say what it or they might be. But the proposition that one is not a toothless brain in a vat, and the like, does not seem to fit into either of these categories. If it can be developed in movie-length detail, it seems too much like an ordinary empirical hypothesis (and why

1. Descartes, *Meditations*, 146.
2. A procedure is sensitive to the truth of a hypothesis if it yields a positive outcome just in case the hypothesis is true. The idea derives from Nozick, whose views on scepticism and knowledge I shall consider in Chapter 5.

should it *not* be treated like an empirical hypothesis?) for one to know it to be true simply because it *is* true, or without there being an answer to the question how one knows this. And since it is not something one is liable to have even considered prior to one's engagement with the sceptical dialectic, one's inability to say how one knows it to be true is not due to the fact that the answer is shrouded in the mists of time.

The apparent lack of any way of coming to know that sceptical hypotheses are false is not, I think, due to an overly restrictive conception of what constitute legitimate ways to come to know things. In Chapter 1 I mentioned Michael Williams's contention that scepticism presupposes a foundationalist epistemology,[3] and suggested that what he might mean by this is not that foundationalism figures as a premise in any sceptical argument—which it does not—but rather that unless one is committed to foundationalism, one will simply not feel the force of the sceptic's premise that one does not know that one is not, say, a brain in a vat. But while it is part of the sceptical hypothesis that one is having all the self-evident beliefs about subjective perceptual experiences one would be having if one were a freshman philosophy student rather than a brain in a vat, I do not see that the acknowledgment that one has no way of refuting this hypothesis presupposes a commitment to the view that any empirical knowledge claim must ultimately be grounded on such experiences. Rather, to use some of the terminology of the last chapter, there do not seem to be *any* relevant and practicable ways or methods that would be generally agreed to be ways or methods for one to establish the falsity of the hypothesis and thereby come to know it. There may indeed be ways for *others* to establish and thereby come to know that one is a freshman philosophy student rather than a brain in a vat, but asking them which it is one is is obviously not a way to come to know this *oneself*, for the answer would be the same whichever one's true situation happened to be. The knowledge that the hypothesis is false simply does not seem available to the individual whose situation it concerns.

The case for the sceptic's premise is reinforced by the consideration of less sweeping sceptical hypotheses that can be adduced in an attempt to undermine ordinary knowledge claims. Consider, for instance, a well-known example of Fred Dretske's: my claim to know that the animals before me in the zoo are zebras might be challenged on the ground that I do not know that they are not mules painted to look like zebras, since I have not undertaken any investigations to establish that they are not.[4] Here the

3. Williams, *Unnatural Doubts*, 51–56.
4. Fred Dretske, "Epistemic Operators," *Journal of Philosophy* 67 (1970), 1007–1023.

hypothesis that they are mules painted to look like zebras is clearly an empirical one, and there *are* ways of coming to know it to be false; it's just that I haven't pursued any of them. The knowledge that they aren't mules may be available to me, but I haven't availed myself of it. Clearly, to say all this does not presuppose any commitment to some particular program in epistemology: *whatever* might constitute legitimate ways of ruling out painted mules, I simply have not taken advantage of them. It might be said that sweeping sceptical hypotheses like the brain-in-a-vat hypothesis differ from the more down-to-earth ones like the mule hypothesis in that there are no ways for one to disprove the former whereas there are ways to disprove the latter; and that this somehow renders the sweeping hypotheses illegitimate. But I think the difference is really a matter of degree. We are asked to regard the brain-in-a-vat hypothesis as on a par with empirical ones, and I can see no convincing reason not to. The claim need not be not that there are no logically possible ways to refute it, or alternatively to discover that one really is a brain in a vat (after all, in *The Matrix* the deception is eventually uncovered). Rather, the claim is just that, upon due consideration, no practicable ways of refuting it seem to be forthcoming, and that in light of this, one must acknowledge that one does not know it to be false.

Let me add one caveat. All this is, it seems to me, perfectly compatible with our regarding the sceptic's hypotheses as ridiculous, with our refusing to engage them, with our dismissing them as absurd, and with our taking it for granted that they are false. Moreover, although I am reluctant to say that we are "entitled" to react to them in these ways (what entitles us?), I would acknowledge that responding to them in these ways would be regarded by most people as entirely appropriate, and I can see no basis for criticizing this general approval of such dismissive reactions to them. But what the sceptic asks us to acknowledge, if we do engage his arguments, is that we have no principled basis for claiming to *know* these hypotheses to be false, and that we do not in fact know them to be false. And it is this acknowledgment that seems difficult to resist.

2. Moore's Response

In a number of well-known writings G. E. Moore suggests that appeals to common sense furnish an adequate response to scepticism, and in particular that an appeal to common sense suffices to rebut the crucial premise of dreaming-type sceptical arguments. Before we consider Moore's response itself, let me note that I am in broad agreement with much of what Moore maintains about knowledge and common sense, and that these areas of agreement constitute an important aspect of the approach to scepticism I am trying to develop in this book. Moore is completely correct, I think, in holding that it is simply obvious to common sense that I know such things as that I have two hands, that I am sitting at my desk, that I have teeth, that I had breakfast this morning, and so on (moreover, I do not think it necessary to precisely delineate the range of these common-sense items of knowledge). I also agree that no sceptical arguments are capable of undermining these common-sense claims to knowledge, in either a psychological or normative sense. To speak of common sense here is not, I take it, to posit a special faculty that furnishes us with a privileged sort of knowledge immune to sceptical challenge (as Thomas Reid may have thought of it). Rather, it is simply a shorthand way of maintaining that some of our beliefs are so obviously true, and so obviously known to be true, that we need supply no detailed justification of them, that we are not to be faulted for maintaining them in the face of sceptical challenges, and that we need not defend them in the face of those challenges. Where I disagree with Moore is in his apparent contention that an appeal to common sense suffices for a straightforward refutation of dreaming-type sceptical arguments, one that establishes the falsity of their crucial premise.

In "Four Forms of Scepticism" Moore says this of a sceptical argument of Bertrand Russell's that rests on four premises or assumptions:

> And what I can't help asking myself in this: Is it, in fact, as certain that all four of these assumptions are true, as that I *do* know that this is a pencil or that you are conscious? I cannot help answering: It seems to me *more* certain that I *do* know that this is a pencil and that you are conscious, than that any single one of these four assumptions are true, let alone all four.[5]

Russell's sceptical argument is not a dreaming-type argument, but in "Certainty" Moore reasons in a similar way about the argument from dreaming:

> I agree, therefore, with that part of the argument which asserts that if I don't know that I'm not dreaming, it follows that I *don't* know that I'm standing up, even if I both actually am and think that I am. But this first part of the argument is a consideration which cuts both ways. For, if it is true, it follows that it is also true that if I *do* know that I am standing up,

5. G. E. Moore, *Philosophical Papers* (London: George Allen & Unwin, 1959), 226.

then I do know that I'm not dreaming. I can therefore just as well argue: since I do know that I'm standing up, it follows that I do know that I'm not dreaming.[6]

Let us take Moore to be offering the following rebuttal of the sceptic's premise that maintains that I do not know that the sceptical hypothesis that I am now dreaming is false:[7] it is obvious to common sense that I know that I am standing up, and nothing could be more certain than that I do know this; and since it follows from this that I know that I am not now dreaming, I do know that I am not now dreaming, contrary to the sceptic's crucial premise.

Now there are some philosophers who find this an acceptable rebuttal of the sceptic's premise.[8] But I think it is fair to say that most, or at least a significant proportion of philosophers interested in scepticism, have not found it convincing. Notice first that on this reading Moore in effect accepts the principle noted in the last section which holds that if I am to know that I am not now dreaming, then there must be some *way* in which I know this (though see below for another reading of Moore). The way in which he claims to know that he is not now dreaming is by inferring it from something he knows with certainty, namely, that he is standing up. But there are at least two difficulties with Moore's response. First, for Moore to come to know that he is not dreaming by inferring it from the fact, which he takes to be obvious, that he knows that he is standing up, it must also be obvious in this sense that the proposition that he knows that he is not dreaming *follows* from the proposition that he knows that he is standing up. Let us grant that it is obvious that I know that I am at my desk. I do not think it can be said to be obvious in this sense that it follows from this, and that I know that it follows from this, that I know that I am not now dreaming. It does follow from it if the transmission principle is valid (with dreaming understood nonveridically), but many philosophers have denied the validity of that principle—we have, after all, found it necessary to consider it at length in Chapter 5. The inference is also valid on Stroud's and Wright's reconstruction of the argument from dreaming we considered in Chapter 1; but since we found reason to reject that reconstruction, it can hardly be said to be obvious that it is a

6. Ibid., 247.
7. Strictly, Moore is talking about what it is rational for me to maintain, but I shall take him to be claiming that I know that the sceptical hypothesis is false.
8. Keith Lehrer seems broadly sympathetic to an approach like Moore's. See his *Thomas Reid* (London: Routledge, 1989), 288–295.

valid one. So the inference Moore relies on does not seem to be a satisfactory way for me to come to know that I am not now dreaming.

The second difficulty with Moore's response is that it ignores the dialectic of our engagement with dreaming-type sceptical arguments I sketched at the beginning of the last section. We begin with something we are confident we know to be true. A hypothesis is then introduced that seems at first unrelated to this item of knowledge, a hypothesis that on reflection we realize we have no way of disproving and thereby coming to know to be false. Finally, we are led to acknowledge that our failure to rule out the sceptical hypothesis undermines our original claim to knowledge. Now Moore's attempt to come to know the sceptic's hypothesis to be false by inference is conceptually *subsequent* to the realization that there is on the face of it no way to disprove the hypothesis, and that knowledge of its falsity is a necessary condition for his possession of the knowledge he initially claimed to have. If he has engaged the sceptic's argument to this point, he is in no position to suddenly announce that he can know the hypothesis to be false by inferring that knowledge from his original, and now undermined, bit of putative knowledge. Were I to claim to know that I've won some publisher's sweepstakes because of apparent assurances to that effect I've received in the mail, and were it then brought to my attention that in order to know that I've won it I would have to know that I'd won a lottery in which the odds against me are staggering, I can't cogently reply that I do know that I've won that lottery, since after all I know I've won the sweepstakes. Maybe I *have* won the lottery, unlikely as it seems. But I can't establish this by simply inferring it from my putative knowledge that I've won the sweepstakes.

It might be said that I have conceded to Moore that its being obvious to common sense that I know that I'm at my desk involves, among other things, that I needn't defend that claim to knowledge against sceptical challenges, and that it isn't undermined by sceptical arguments. Why then can't I base a refutation of the crucial premise of the sceptic's arguments on that knowledge, since it isn't undermined by those arguments? The problem is that this assumes that the reason that my common-sense claim to knowledge is not undermined by the sceptic's arguments is that the arguments are unsound because of a false premise. Yet it may be that they do not undermine the claim because they are invalid, or because of the nature of the concept of knowledge and of the delicate relation between particular arguments and rules of inference (the view I am trying to develop here). Moreover, although I am not to be faulted for simply ignoring the sceptic's arguments and continuing to maintain that I know that I am at my desk, to engage them in the way I've indicated (which is the way in which Moore seems to engage them) seems to me to *concede* to the sceptic that his arguments are capable of undermining my common-sense claims to knowledge, a concession incompatible with Moore's strategy.

There may be another way to try to fashion a refutation of sceptical hypotheses out of Moore's appeal to common sense, and that is to read him as maintaining (or at least as leaving open the possibility) that the propositions that one is not dreaming, not a brain in a vat, and so on are themselves among the propositions which it is obvious to common sense we know to be true and for which we need supply no detailed justification or account of how we know them. I do not think that this is what Moore intended, though the fact that in "A Defence of Common Sense" he includes the proposition that the Earth has existed for many years before his body was born among the propositions of common sense, together with the fact that Russell once formulated a sceptical hypothesis to the effect that the world with all its fossils and apparent memories came into existence five minutes ago, might tempt some to think otherwise.[9] But in any event I do not think that this strategy is a tenable one: for as I indicated in the last section, an important fact about sceptical hypotheses is that they are *surprising,* seeming at first unrelated to the things common sense takes us to know, of dubious intelligibility, and not the sort of things common sense has considered or rendered a verdict on. But let me defer further consideration of this way of dealing with sceptical hypotheses until the next section, where I want to consider a strategy suggested by Wittgenstein's remarks on Moore's response to scepticism.

3. A POSSIBLE WITTGENSTEINIAN RESPONSE

The late compilation *On Certainty* consists of remarks resulting from Wittgenstein's reflections on Moore's response to scepticism. Wittgenstein thought that the kinds of common-sense propositions Moore claims to know to be true in an effort to rebut the sceptic's premise are of considerable importance, though not for the reason Moore takes them to be:

> That is why Moore's assurance that he knows . . . does not interest us. The propositions, however, which Moore retails as examples of such known truths are indeed interesting. Not because anyone knows their truth, or be-

9. Moore, *Philosophical Papers*, 29. Bertrand Russell, *The Analysis of Mind* (London: George Allen & Unwin, 1921), 159.

lieves he knows them, but because they all have a *similar* role in the system of our empirical judgements.[10]

Their role is sketched in remarks like this:

> That is to say, the *questions* that they raise and our *doubts* depend on the fact that some propositions are exempt from doubt, are as it were like hinges on which those turn.

> That is to say, it belongs to the logic of our scientific investigations that certain things are *in deed* [*sic*] not doubted.

> But it isn't that the situation is like this: We just *can't* investigate everything, and for that reason we are forced to rest content with assumption. If we want the door to turn, the hinges must stay put.[11]

Wittgenstein's thought is that the special role of what have come to be called "hinge" propositions (the common-sense truisms to which Moore calls attention) is that taking them for granted, accepting them without investigation, allows the activity of empirical investigation—inquiring into, establishing, verifying, and refuting *other* propositions—to take place. Moreover, taking them for granted or accepting them as a matter of course is, as a matter of fact, a precondition for learning "language games" or acquiring the concepts embedded in those games:

> For how can a child immediately doubt what it is taught? That could only mean that he was incapable of learning certain language games.[12]
> We teach a child "that is your hand", not "that is perhaps [or "probably"] your hand". That is how a child learns the innumerable language-games that are concerned with his hand. An investigation or question, 'whether this is really a hand' never occurs to him. Nor, on the other hand, does he learn that he *knows* that this is a hand.[13]

Some philosophers have been tempted to find in Wittgenstein's remarks about the special role of hinge propositions the seeds of a rebuttal of the sceptic's crucial premise. Michael Williams, though he does not try to extract a rebuttal of scepticism from Wittgenstein's remarks, suggests

---

10. Ludwig Wittgenstein, *On Certainty*, ed. G. E. M. Anscombe and G. H. von Wright, trans. Denis Paul and G. E. M. Anscombe (Oxford: Basil Blackwell, 1969), sec. 137.
11. Ibid., secs. 341–343.
12. Ibid., sec. 283.
13. Ibid., sec. 374.

that certain propositions' exemption from doubt is *logically* required by the character of inquiry, and that this affects the epistemic status of the propositions that are so exempt.[14] Crispin Wright does suggest that a response to sceptical arguments may be fashioned from some extension of Wittgenstein's views, for he take him to be maintaining that hinge propositions, by virtue of their special role, are justified or warranted for us even though we have done nothing to establish them and have no particular reasons or evidence in their favor,[15] and thus may be deployed against the sceptic:

> What [their certainty] is based on is their possession, in contexts in which they are the termini of evidence chains, of a quasi-normative role: they are absolved from doubt just in so far as our practice does not admit of their being doubted. . . . The mistake of a sceptic about the certainty of these propositions, so used, is to draw the wrong conclusion from the absence of anything we can point to as a sufficient *cognitive* basis for the certainty attached to them. What constitutes their certainty is merely the high priority assigned to them by our rules of procedure.[16]

One difficulty with trying to fashion a response to the sceptic's premise from what Wittgenstein says in *On Certainty* is the fact that, as I noted in the last section, the hinge propositions with which Wittgenstein is concerned are basically the common-sense propositions enumerated by Moore, and these do not explicitly include the negations of traditional sceptical hypotheses. But Moore's propositions do include the denial of Russell's sceptical hypothesis that the world came into existence five minutes ago, complete with fossils, historical records, and pseudomemories. And Wittgenstein does imagine a schoolboy who keeps wondering if the table he is being taught the word for continues to exist when he turns around or when no one sees it.[17] So in the interest of exploring the possible Wittgensteinian response to scepticism, let us, with Wright,[18] allow that the denials of sceptical hypotheses may be among the propositions we simply take for granted in our investigative and linguistic practices.

Another difficulty with bringing Wright's Wittgensteinian response to bear on the kind of sceptical arguments at issue here is that hinge propo-

---

14. Williams, *Unnatural Doubts*, 123.
15. Crispin Wright, "Facts and Certainty," *Proceedings of the British Academy* 71 (1985), 450, and "Dreaming and Scepticism," 104.
16. Wright, "Facts and Certainty," 469–470.
17. Wittgenstein, *On Certainty*, sec. 314.
18. Wright, "Dreaming and Scepticism," 87n, 104.

sitions, including the denials of sceptical hypotheses, are, according to him, *warranted* or *reasonable* to believe in the absence of any investigation of them; and the sceptical arguments he is interested in are, as we saw in Chapter 1, ones that try to establish that our everyday beliefs are not *reasonable* or *warranted*. Our arguments, though, attempt to establish that we do not *know* these beliefs to be true, and the premise at issue here is that we do not *know* sceptical hypotheses to be false. But again, in the interest of exploring the response, let us take Wright to be suggesting that by virtue of their special role, hinge propositions, including the denial of sceptical hypotheses, are *known* to be true, even though there is no particular *way*, or answer to the question of *how*, we know them to be true (this response thus denies the principle supporting the sceptic's premise, that if we are to know sceptical hypotheses to be false, there must be some way in which we have come to know this). There is in fact some basis for this reading of Wright, for he takes Wittgenstein to maintain that hinge propositions are *certain* in a nonpsychological sense, and seems to leave it open whether this kind of certainty might be taken to encompass both warranted belief and knowledge.[19]

The first problem with this response is that, whatever its intrinsic merits, it is not Wittgenstein's view, and in fact turns Wittgenstein's view on its head. Wittgenstein thought that Moore's response to scepticism was a "mistake,"[20] not just in its particulars but in his attempt to engage scepticism directly at all. I take it that Wittgenstein was not offering *another* direct response to scepticism, and indeed I would go so far as to say that *On Certainty* is not even primarily a work about epistemology. Rather, what interested him about Moore's response was the common-sense propositions Moore adduced and the special role they play in our practices of inquiry in particular and in our linguistic practices generally. And his overall point is that, contrary to Moore's insistence that he knows them to be true, the fact that these hinge propositions play this role requires only that we take them for granted, and does *not* require them to be antecedently known or to have some privileged epistemic status; nor does this role confer any privileged epistemic status on them:

> "So one must know that the objects whose names one teaches a child by an ostensive definition exist."—Why must one know they do? Isn't it enough that experience doesn't later show the opposite?
> For why should the language-game rest on some kind of knowledge?[21]

19. Wright, "Facts and Certainty," 470–471.
20. Wittgenstein, *On Certainty*, sec. 521.
21. Ibid., sec. 477.

Wittgenstein often insists that he is simply describing aspects of our practices, and I think it is especially important to take him at his word here. He is not of course denying that we do sometimes know the sorts of things Moore claims to know. What he is calling attention to is the fact that in relying on hinge propositions we merely take them for granted—"it belongs to the logic of our scientific investigations that certain things are *in deed* [*sic*] not doubted"[22]—and that, as the previous remark maintains, they successfully play their role as long as that reliance is not embarrassed by experience, even though we typically do not know them to be true, not having investigated them at all. As he says in a remark quoted earlier, an "investigation or question 'whether this is really a hand' never occurs" to a child being taught the meaning of the word 'hand,' and the child does not thereby learn that he knows that this is a real hand.[23]

But it might be said that even though a response along Wright's lines is not to be found in Wittgenstein's writings, we can arrive at such a response by building on his remarks. For it might be argued that if in our investigative practices we do rely, as Wittgenstein says, on hinge propositions, then the results of those practices qualify as knowledge only if we know the hinge propositions presupposed by those practices to be true. And it might then be further argued that since our ordinary investigative practices typically *do* furnish us with knowledge, the hinge practices they presuppose are known to be true by virtue of their special role in our acquisition of knowledge.

This line of reasoning, which has a transcendental air about it, seems to me quite hopeless, both on its own and as a response to the sceptic's arguments. The claim that the results of our epistemic practices amount to knowledge only if all the propositions presupposed by those practices are known to be true resembles Stroud's principle in Chapter 1 to the effect that one knows that p only if one knows to obtain every condition one knows to be necessary for knowing that p. This principle, it will be recalled, is the basis for one reconstruction of dreaming-type arguments (though a reconstruction I argued was unsatisfactory). Wittgenstein's assessment of the role of hinge propositions in our practices of inquiry ought, I think, to lead us to reject both the claim and the principle it resembles. But if we do accept the claim, then the obvious reply for the sceptic is to maintain that our ordinary epistemic practices do *not* furnish us with knowledge, since we do *not* know to be true the denials of sceptical hypotheses those practices presuppose. And if at this point we counter

22. Ibid., sec. 342.
23. Ibid., sec. 374.

that since those practices *do* furnish us with knowledge, the denials of sceptical hypotheses *are* known to be true by virtue of their being presupposed by those practices, we are simply back at Moore's response: we *must* know that sceptical hypotheses are false, since if we did not know this we would not know other things we do know. We have already seen the inadequacy of that response, a response Wittgenstein himself rejected as a "mistake." The proposal we have been considering tries to extract from Wittgenstein's writings a response to scepticism which is not only strikingly similar to one he explicitly rejects, but seems unsatisfactory in its own right.

4. A COHERENTIST RESPONSE

In the Sixth Meditation Descartes rules out the dreaming hypothesis of the First Meditation on the grounds that his belief that he is indeed awake completely coheres with all his other beliefs, experiences, and memories. Of course this appeal to coherence is made only after he thinks he has secured a divine guarantee that carefully scrutinized and maximally coherent beliefs are true; but it might be thought that considerations of coherence can be used to refute the sceptic's premise even in the absence of a divine guarantee. Perhaps the most promising form for an appeal to coherence to take is that of an inference to the best explanation. In *The Problems of Philosophy* Russell writes:

> There is no logical impossibility in the supposition that the whole of life is a dream, in which we ourselves create all the objects that come before us. But although this is not logically impossible, there is no reason whatever to suppose that it is true; and it is, in fact, a less simple hypothesis, viewed as a means of accounting for the facts of our own life, than the common-sense hypothesis that there really are objects independent of us, whose action on us causes our sensations.[24]

And similar appeals to an inference to the best explanation to rule out sceptical hypotheses have been made more recently by Peter Strawson and Jonathan Vogel.[25] The basic strategy is this. Consider a "neutral" de-

24. Russell, *Problems of Philosophy*, 22–23. Russell does not actually claim to establish that we know the sceptical hypothesis to be false: he says that the argument is less strong than we would like, and that the dreaming hypothesis remains a possibility. But for purposes of discussion I will take him to be making the stronger claim.
25. Peter Strawson, *Skepticism and Naturalism: Some Varieties* (London: Methuen, 1985),

scription E of my subjective experiences, thoughts, feelings, memories, and so on, a description that is presumed to exhibit a high degree of pattern and order. Then consider two mutually exclusive and exhaustive hypotheses for explaining E: R, which incorporates the common-sense beliefs under sceptical attack, together with appropriate psychological and physical laws and mechanisms for producing the experiences and thoughts described in E; and a sweeping sceptical hypothesis SH, which says that R (including the common-sense beliefs it incorporates) is false and that my experiences and thoughts are brought about in *some* way other than the one described by R, a way that nevertheless brings about exactly the experiences and thoughts I would have if R were true. (Notice that this formulation of SH differs from those introduced earlier, which specified a particular way—dreams, demons, etc.—my experiences and thoughts are supposed to arise. This makes R and SH exclusive and exhaustive, unlike the earlier versions.) It is then argued that SH can be known to be false on the grounds that R provides a vastly superior explanation of E than does SH.

Although some philosophers have been drawn to this response to the sceptic's crucial premise, I think it is fair to say that, as with Moore's response, most of those interested in scepticism have not found it persuasive. The reasons for this are not hard to see. First, there is almost no consensus as to what constitutes a "best" explanation and how such criteria should be applied to sceptical hypotheses.[26] Second, the quasi-foundationalist assumption that there is available a "neutral" description E, not couched in material or physical terms, of our subjective experiences and thoughts is widely regarded as unfounded.[27] And finally, it is simply not the case that we come by our knowledge of our common-sense beliefs about our surroundings by making such an inference, for it is not possible even for psychologists of perception and neuroscientists, let alone the man on the street, to formulate the supposed explanation R of the experiences and thoughts supposedly described by E.

While I think that these are indeed sufficient grounds for rejecting this version of the coherentist response to the sceptic's premise, I think there

---

429; Jonathan Vogel, "Cartesian Skepticism and Inference to the Best Explanation," *Journal of Philosophy* 87 (1990), 658–666.

26. Vogel offers some pertinent proposals in "Cartesian Skepticism," but their shortcomings are brought out by Berent Enc in "Is Realism Really the Best Hypothesis?" (abstract), *Journal of Philosophy* 87 (1990), 667–668.

27. See, for example, Wright, "Facts and Certainty," 447–449, and Michael Williams, *Groundless Belief* (Oxford: Basil Blackwell, 1975), 429 n. 1, 140–141.

is also reason to find the response unsatisfactory even if the explanatory criteria, the neutral description E, and the proposed explanation R were forthcoming. The suspicion is that the sweeping nature of sceptical hypotheses, and the fact that they are specifically formulated to preserve whatever patterns and order our experiences and beliefs exhibit, mean that considerations of explanatory superiority can find no foothold here, even though such considerations may indeed be relevant for deciding among ordinary competing empirical hypotheses. If its explanatory inferiority enables us to know that the sweeping sceptical hypothesis SH described above is false, we need some assurance, in lieu of Descartes' divine guarantee, that if the realist explanation R best explains E, it is more *likely* to be true than SH:

(1) $Pr(R|R$ best explains $E) > Pr(SH|R$ best explains $E)$.

Now if the sceptical hypothesis is formulated in the sweeping manner indicated above, R and SH are mutually exclusive and exhaustive (as they would have to be if R's explanatory superiority to SH is to suffice for us to know R to be true):

(2) $R \equiv \neg SH$.

And from this follow

(3) $Pr(R$ best explains $E|R) = Pr(R$ best explains $E|\neg SH)$
(4) $Pr(R$ best explains $E|\neg R) = Pr(R$ best explains $E|SH)$.

(In the case of ordinary competing empirical hypotheses, (2), and hence (3) and (4), would not hold.) Moreover, SH has been specifically formulated to preserve the order, coherence, and relations of explanatory superiority among our experiences and beliefs, and so

(5) $Pr(R$ best explains $E|R) = Pr(R$ best explains $E|SH)$.

Given all this, when we use Bayes' theorem to calculate the required inequality (1), we find that it reduces to

(6) $Pr(R) > Pr(SH)$.

This means that the explanatory superiority of R over SH renders it no more likely than SH to be true than it is in the absence of this superiority.

The sceptic may deny that R is initially more likely to be true than SH; or he may be willing to concede that it is. In either case, his claim is simply that we do not *know* SH to be false. And what the foregoing argument shows is that appealing in addition to considerations of explanatory superiority will not suffice for us to know this either.

We can broaden the argument to undermine coherentist responses to the sceptic's premise generally. If we replace 'R best explains E' in (1)–(5) with something like 'R maximally coheres with our other beliefs,' (3)–(5) remain true (this generalized version makes the special character of sceptical hypotheses even more apparent, for the new version of (5) would typically not hold if R and SH were replaced by ordinary empirical hypotheses). So (1) still reduces to (6). Thus the initial suspicion that considerations of coherence would not, because of the special character of sceptical hypotheses, furnish us with grounds for rejecting the sceptic's contention that we do not know these hypotheses to be false seems to be borne out.

5. THE CONTEXTUALIST RESPONSE

Perhaps the subtlest strategy for denying the sceptic's premise is the view called *contextualism,* versions of which have been formulated by Peter Unger, David Lewis, Stuart Cohen, and Keith DeRose.[28] The basic idea behind contextualism (which seems to me to derive from Norman Malcolm's attempt to draw a distinction between a strong and a weak sense of 'know'[29]) is that the epistemic standards that determine the truth of the proposition expressed by a sentence containing the word 'know' depend on the context of discourse in which the sentence is used. In "ordinary" contexts in which scepticism and sceptical hypotheses are not at issue, these standards are low enough that it is true to assert that I know, say, that I have teeth; and it is also true that I know that the kind of sceptical hypotheses we have been discussing are false. But in the context of a con-

28. Peter Unger, *Philosophical Relativity* (Minneapolis: University of Minnesota Press, 1983), and "The Cone Model of Knowledge," *Philosophical Topics* 14 (1986), 125–178; David Lewis, "Elusive Knowledge," *Australasian Journal of Philosophy* 74 (1996), 549–567; Stewart Cohen, "Knowledge, Context, and Social Standards," *Synthèse* 73 (1987), 3–26, and "How to Be a Fallabilist," *Philosophical Perspectives* 2 (1988), 91–123; DeRose, "Solving the Skeptical Problem" and "Contextualism and Knowledge Attributions," *Philosophy and Phenomenological Research* 52 (1992), 913–929.

29. Norman Malcolm, "Knowledge and Belief," in *Knowledge and Certainty* (Englewood Cliffs, N.J.: Prentice-Hall, 1963).

sideration of scepticism—a context created, for example, by an assertion or a denial that one knows a sceptical hypothesis to be false (or the mere entertainment of a thought to that effect—see note 34)—these standards are raised to such a degree that the proposition expressed by an assertoric use of 'I know that I have teeth' becomes false, as does a claim to know the sceptical hypothesis to be false. The word 'know' is thus comparable to a word like 'flat': what one says by the use of 'This surface is flat' may be true in the context of a discussion of a football field but false in the context of an experiment involving low-friction ball bearings.

What is attractive about the contextualist strategy is that it seems to account for both the seductiveness of sceptical arguments and the fact that they seem powerless to undermine our common-sense claims to knowledge. They are seductive because in the context created by their mere consideration they are indeed sound, leading from true premises to a true conclusion. But the conclusion expressed by 'I do not know that I have teeth' in that context is not incompatible with the claim expressed by 'I know that I have teeth' used outside the context of Hume's study, where that claim is true (and where it is false that I do not know the sceptical hypothesis to be false, so that the sceptic's arguments are unsound), and its truth is unaffected by what is said in the sceptical context.

Since DeRose's version of contextualism seems to me the most developed, it is the one I shall consider here, though most of what I shall say about it applies to other versions as well. DeRose applies contextualism to the following dream-type argument, which he calls the *argument from ignorance* (AI) (here H is a sceptical hypothesis and O a proposition that common sense says one knows to be true):

    (1) I don't know that not-H.
    (2) If I don't know that not-H, then I don't know that O.
    ———
    (3) I don't know that O.[30]

The problem is to explain both why this argument seems compelling and why common sense is not mistaken in holding that one knows O to be true. DeRose's solution appeals to what he calls the *rule of sensitivity*, which he claims governs the epistemic standards by which knowledge claims are to be evaluated. One's belief that p is *insensitive* just in case one would have it even if p were false, and *sensitive* otherwise. Sensitivity is

30. DeRose, "Solving the Skeptical Problem," 1.

thus a modal notion, and can be further explicated in terms of possible worlds: one's belief that p is sensitive just in case, roughly, one fails to have it in the epistemically relevant possible worlds in which p is false and one has it in the relevant worlds in which p is true.[31] Assuming that p is true in the actual world, the sphere of relevant possible worlds contains roughly those worlds closest to the actual world in which p is false, together with those worlds closer than these in which p is true. The rule of sensitivity can be formulated in these two ways:

> When it is asserted that some subject S knows (or does not know) some proposition P, the standards for knowledge (the standards for how good an epistemic position one must be in to count as knowing) tend to be raised, if need be, to such a level as to require S's belief in that particular P to be sensitive for it to count as knowledge.[32]

> When it's asserted that S knows (or doesn't know) that P, then, if necessary, enlarge the sphere of epistemically relevant worlds so that it at least includes the closest worlds in which P is false.[33]

Now consider the argument AI. According to the rule of sensitivity, in the context of discourse created by the sceptic's assertion of its first premise (or by its mere consideration),[34] the epistemic standards are raised to a level at which one knows not-H only if one's belief that not-H is sensitive—that is, only if it covaries with the truth of not-H throughout the very large sphere of epistemically relevant worlds. But one's belief that not-H is *not* sensitive, since the hypothesis is so constructed that one would believe it to be false even if it were true, and so one does not know that not-H and the first premise is true. Assuming the truth of the second premise,[35] it follows that one does not know that O. And indeed at the

---

31. DeRose draws the rule of sensitivity from Nozick's account of knowledge, which I shall discuss in Chapter 5.

32. DeRose, "Solving the Skeptical Problem," 36.

33. Ibid., 37.

34. Though DeRose usually speaks of a context being created by an assertion (or a denial) of AI's premise, it seems clear that for his view to be of interest the contextualist must hold that the mere discussion or consideration of the premise, or of AI as a whole, is sufficient to create the context. Similarly, it seems clear that the consideration or discussion need not be verbal: merely considering or entertaining the thought of the premise or the argument—as Descartes originally did—suffices to create the context.

35. There is an oddity about DeRose's reconstruction of the dreaming-type argument AI. He does not derive the second premise, as one might expect, from some version of the transmission principle or from what, following Wright, we called Descartes' principle in Chapter 1. Rather, he bases it on the intuition that not-H and O are on an epistemic par, or

high standards induced by the sceptic's assertion of the first premise, one does *not* know that O, for one's belief that O does not covary with the truth of O throughout the large sphere of relevant possible worlds. But in the everyday contexts outside Hume's study, claims to know that O are, according to the rule of sensitivity, properly evaluated by epistemic standards requiring one's belief that O to be sensitive to count as knowledge. And in these contexts it *is* sensitive, for one has it in the (now much fewer) relevant possible worlds in which O is true, and fails to have it in the relevant worlds in which O is false; and so one does know that O. And by these (low) standards, one knows that not-H as well, and the first premise of AI is false. It's just that the *assertion* (or consideration) of the first premise creates a context in which the proposition asserted is true. But in everyday contexts, in which the first premise of AI is not in the picture, the proposition expressed by that premise is false.

DeRose also offers an explanation of why, despite the seductiveness of AI, we have a tendency to resist the conclusion and maintain that we know that O. The explanation is that we dimly realize that as soon as we are back in the sort of ordinary context in which we do know that O, the sceptic's denial that we know it will be false; and we confuse this with the claim that this denial is false now, in the context induced by AI.[36]

Before assessing contextualism itself, let me indicate that as a response to scepticism it strikes me as a nonstarter. DeRose suggests that the claim that at the high standards supposedly induced by AI I don't know that O is an innocuous one, and that this sort of timid scepticism does not seriously conflict with common sense. This seems to me to be just wrong. On my view it is simply obvious that I know that I have teeth or have parents, and there is *no* legitimate sense of 'know' or legitimate standards for evaluating knowledge claims according which I do not know these things. The idea that timid scepticism is innocuous seems to me akin to the old positivist view that no empirical proposition can ever be "theo-

---

that one is in no better position to know the latter than to know the former ("Solving the Skeptical Problem," 29–33). This seems to distort the dialectic of the consideration of dreaming-type arguments I discussed at the beginning of this chapter. What is so surprising about the sceptic's argument in the first place is the way it draws a connection between a proposition like "I'm not a brain in a vat, etc.," which on reflection one realizes one is in no position to establish, and a proposition like "I have teeth," which seems like a paradigm example of the sort of thing one *is* in a position to know to be true. DeRose bases his claim that not-H and O are on an epistemic par on the alleged fact that one readily assents to the conditional "If I don't know that not-H, I don't know that O." But there is a circularity here, for he then bases his acceptance of this conditional on the alleged epistemic parity of not-H and O.

36. DeRose, "Solving the Skeptical Problem," 40–41.

retically certain" (a position whose air of absurdity was not dispelled by the word 'theoretically'), and to Wright's view, noted in Chapter 1, that a form of scepticism concerning only knowledge rather than warranted belief is harmless and simply invites a "Russellian retreat" in which we concede that we don't really possess knowledge in some impractically strict sense. But from my vantage point, conceding that the sceptic's claims are true according to strict but nevertheless legitimate standards doesn't really dispose of the problem of scepticism at all.

I think that there is more than just a brute clash of intuitions here, and that the idea that there is some legitimate sense of 'know' in which I don't know that I have hands can be traced to two fallacious assumptions. The first is that since there is, as I concede below, some basis for contextualism, in that *some* propositions are such that we regard them as known to be true in some contexts (e.g., casual conversations) but not in others (e.g., a courtroom), it must be the case that *all* propositions are such that there are contexts in which they are not known to be true. But this generalization of this truth about the kinds of ordinary examples that motivate contextualism to cover all knowledge claims is simply unwarranted. The second fallacy concerns possibility. The idea that there is such a strict sense of 'know' can be traced to the idea that there is at least the bare *possibility* that I don't have hands, and that knowledge in the strictest sense is incompatible with this bare possibility. Historically, this line of reasoning often involved confusing logical and epistemic possibility, as in the positivists' insistence that contingent propositions could never be theoretically certain. I am not suggesting that present-day contextualists are guilty of this confusion, but I do think that there is a lingering tendency to suppose that free-floating *epistemic* possibilities are simply there to be appealed to in order to undermine ordinary knowledge claims, including the claim that I know that I have hands. But on the view of knowledge and possibility I defended in Chapter 2, knowledge and epistemic possibility are duals, and the claim that there is an epistemic possibility that I don't have hands is simply equivalent to the claim that my having hands is not (available to be) known, and thus cannot be appealed to in order to undermine the latter claim.

How plausible is DeRose's sort of contextualism in its own right? As I just noted, *some* form of contextualism is highly plausible, for it does seem that our willingness to make knowledge claims varies with the circumstances and with what is at stake or what hangs on the truth of the claim. A knowledge claim I might make in the course of a casual conversation might be one I would be more hesitant to make in a courtroom or laboratory; and this might suggest that the epistemic standards appropriate to evaluating knowledge claims vary with their context.[37] But in these cases what creates the different putative contexts are factors like what hangs on the outcome of our deliberations in them, or what is at stake in those deliberations. These contexts are created by our interests and purposes, and all parties to the deliberations can be presumed to realize, say, that stricter epistemic standards are appropriate to a murder trial than to a backyard discussion of current affairs. But DeRose's sort of contextualism is quite different, for what is supposed to create the different contexts of discourse is the *subject matter* of the propositions being discussed. What induces the context appropriate to an evaluation of sceptical arguments is not the fact that we are in, say, a philosophy seminar room, but the fact that the *content* of sceptical hypotheses requires all knowledge claims under consideration to be evaluated with respect to a much larger sphere of possible worlds than they would be if the sceptical hypotheses had not been introduced.[38] This has some rather peculiar consequences, but before we turn to them let me call attention to a related point raised by Stephen Shiffer: that contextualists like DeRose lack a plausible explanation of how speakers using the term 'know' can so often be mistaken about what they are actually saying.[39] There are, Shiffer notes, expressions that are genuinely contextual. These include "hidden indexicals" like 'It's raining' (which can be used to say that it's raining here *in Milwaukee*). But normal users of expressions like this are perfectly aware of their indexical nature and are hardly apt to use them to actually say, for example, that it's raining in Milwaukee, while mistakenly thinking that they were saying that it's raining in Chicago. Vague terms like 'flat' are also genuinely contextual: to call a football field flat is to say something quite different about it than to call the highly polished surface of some experimental apparatus flat. But again, typical users of such terms are perfectly aware of this, and are under no illusions that in applying the term

37. Alternatively, one might hold that the epistemic standards appropriate to knowledge claims are invariant, but that in the casual conversation one is speaking loosely, and that what one says is not literally true. In *Philosophical Relativity* Unger argues that the choice between this view and the contextualist view is indeterminate.

38. Of course, our interests in making or considering knowledge claims may be relevant to what the context is (e.g., is it a philosophical discussion or not?). But the point is that given, say, that our interests are philosophical, what the context is depends on the content of the propositions under consideration.

39. Shiffer, "Contextualist Solutions to Scepticism." My overall view of scepticism is similar to Shiffer's in some respects, as he takes it to present a genuine paradox. But he characterizes the paradox—or what I prefer to call the anomaly—of scepticism differently than I do.

to the two surfaces one is saying the same thing about them. And the same is true of the plausible sort of contextualism involving 'know': if different epistemic standards are appropriate to the courtroom than to the backyard, typical users of the term can be presumed to be aware of this.

But contextualists like DeRose have to hold that in using 'know' speakers are often grossly mistaken about what they are saying: someone denying the conclusion of AI is simply confusing the proposition expressed by 'I don't know that O' in the context created by that argument with the proposition it would express in the context of an ordinary conversation. DeRose's explanation—that such a person is dimly aware that the sentence could be used to say something false in the latter context and is thereby fooled into thinking that it is being used to say something false in the former—seems contrived and unconvincing. Competent users of genuinely contextual terms aren't prone to such wholesale confusion, and it is hard to see why they should fall into it when the talk turns to knowledge.

The rule of sensitivity seems to operate rather selectively. The assertion or entertainment of the first premise of AI is said to expand the sphere of relevant worlds in such a way that this premise becomes true. One wonders then why, according to the rule, the assertion or consideration of the conclusion of AI doesn't contract the sphere of relevant worlds in such a way that the conclusion becomes false.[40] Apparently the contexts created by a consideration of whether one knows a sceptical hypothesis to be false are durable ones, which persist throughout the entire conversational setting in which the question is raised. This has peculiar consequences. It would, for example, allow the defense in a trial to undermine the prosecution's attempt to establish certain facts by having a sceptical philosopher testify that he doesn't know that he's not a brain in a vat ('The defense calls to the stand Peter Unger'), thereby creating a context in which witnesses can't truthfully claim to know the defendant's whereabouts on the night of the crime.[41]

David Lewis acknowledges that (his version of) contextualism has consequences of this sort, but tries to render them less counterintuitive by proposing that our minds are "compartmentalized," so that in the courtroom example the compartment attending to the judicial proceeding would pay no attention to the sceptic's testimony, which would be attended to only by the philosophical compartment.[42] While this strikes me

40. This is roughly Nozick's position.
41. I owe this example to Mark Kaplan.
42. Lewis, "Elusive Knowledge," 559–560, 565.

as implausible on its face, it might be suggested more broadly that since the sceptic's testimony is, in some sense to be made out, inappropriate to a judicial proceeding, it does not alter the context in which the latter takes place. This will not alleviate the problem, though, for contextualism allows everyday knowledge claims to be undermined by the consideration of ordinary empirical hypotheses that are entirely appropriate to their settings. Recall the hypothesis R from the last section, which purports to explain how our subjective experiences and beliefs are caused by our interaction with our external environment. Suppose that at a cognitive science seminar we are discussing an apparently reasonable hypothesis R* that purports to explain how our beliefs arise in response to our environment, a hypothesis that some at the seminar suggest may possibly be mistaken despite its plausibility. Suppose not only that R* is false, but that it is radically enough mistaken that if it were true the beliefs about our environment generated by our interaction with it would be mostly false. According to DeRose, raising the possibility of R*'s falsehood expands the sphere of relevant possible worlds to include worlds in which R* is true, thereby creating a context in which in order to count as knowledge, our ordinary beliefs about our environment must covary with truths about our environment throughout this large sphere of possible worlds. But given the nature of R*, our beliefs about our environment don't satisfy this requirement (since if R* were true they would be mostly false), so that while we are at the seminar we don't know that we are there, that we are sitting at a table, that we are wearing pants, and so on. This consequence is absurd, and yet R* is a perfectly appropriate subject of consideration in such a setting.

The way in which the content of knowledge claims (or denials) creates the contexts in which they are to be evaluated has further consequences that render contextualism of dubious coherence, for it places severe restrictions on what can be said or thought. It is supposed to be true in ordinary contexts that I know that I'm not a brain in a vat; but I can never truly *say* that I know this, for to make that assertion automatically creates a context in which it is false. Contextualism is supposed to account for the power of sceptical arguments while reassuring us that our common-sense claims to knowledge are true; but this reassurance is hollow, for I can never say or think, for instance, that unlike the poor souls in *The Matrix,* I at least know what my real condition is. Similarly, contextualism assures us that in ordinary contexts the argument AI is unsound; but we can never say or think this, for to do so creates a context in which AI is sound.

DeRose's explanation of our tendency to deny the conclusion of AI appeals to our realization that in ordinary contexts the sentence expressing that conclusion—"I don't know that O"—could be used to say something true. But while in the context induced by AI, I *can't* say or think that although I don't now know that I have teeth, yesterday I did know this and I will know it again tomorrow (in ordinary contexts). As DeRose makes clear, contextualists have to hold that all uses of 'know,' whether in the past, present, or future tense, are governed by the context one is presently in.[43] In the context induced by AI all I can truly say is that I don't know that I have teeth and that I never knew this and never will know this. Moreover, since—contextualism aside—it is unintelligible for me to say that while I don't know that p, nevertheless others know it, in the context induced by AI not only must I say that I don't know that there are trees, I must also say that no one knows this and that no one ever has or ever will.

We might try to salvage some of the reassurance contextualism seeks to provide by noting that according to DeRose, while I cannot now (in the context of a consideration of scepticism) say or think that while I don't know that I have teeth, I knew it yesterday and will know it tomorrow (or that people know there are trees), I *can* say or think that yesterday I could, and tomorrow I will again be able to, use the sentence 'I know that I have teeth' (or 'People know that there are trees') to say something true. But even this reassurance is illusory. The sentence 'I know that p' (or 'People know that p') is factive and entails that it is true that p. Thus if I say that while I don't know that p, there are contexts in which I can use the sentence 'I know that p' (or 'People know that p') to say something true, my assertion involves me in the claim that it is true that p though I don't know that p. But this is a claim I can never be in a position to make, for it shares the character of the statements constituting Moore's paradox—which came up in the last chapter—such as that it is raining, though I don't believe that it is.[44] The reason I can't say that even though I don't know that p, someone else knows it is that this involves me in the claim that it is true that p though I don't know it, a claim that I can never be in a position to make. If I am to say or think that even though I don't now know that I

43. DeRose, "Contextualism and Knowledge Attributions," 925–927.

44. Williamson would agree, independently of considerations involving Moore's paradox, for he holds that one must know that p in order to be in a position to assert that p (see *Knowledge and Its Limits,* chap. 11). But one need not share Williamson's rather strong position—which entails that one can never be in a position to assert a falsehood—to agree that one can never be in a position to assert that p while maintaining that one does not know that p (see the brief discussion of Moore's paradox in the last chapter).

have teeth, I can sometimes use the sentence 'I know that I have teeth' to say something true, I must be in a position to say that I have teeth though I don't know that I do. But this is something I can never be in a position to say.

Finally, even if this problem could be avoided,[45] and I could now in my study say that the man on the street or my earlier self says something true in uttering the sentence 'I know that I have teeth,' or expresses a true thought in uttering it, I can't say *what* he says or thinks (for instance, that he knows that he has teeth). Thus the promise contextualism holds out of allowing us to say in the context of the study that the common-sense epistemological assertions and thoughts of those outside that context are correct is a hollow one, for we can have no idea what such people say or think (just as we might be able to say that the speakers of some language we don't understand are making true assertions without having any idea what they are saying).

The contextualist response to the sceptic's crucial premise thus seems to me unsatisfactory on a number of grounds: it does not provide a satisfactory response to scepticism even if true; it implies that we do not know things in contexts in which we obviously do know them; and the reassurances it seeks to provide regarding our knowledge in ordinary contexts are unintelligible.

In this chapter I've surveyed what seem to me to be the most important strategies for responding to sceptical arguments by denying one or more of their premises. While I certainly wouldn't claim to have conclusively refuted all of these strategies, that fact that each of them is open to serious objections, together with the fact that scepticism continues to persist as a philosophical problem, suggests that this kind of response to sceptical arguments is unlikely to succeed.

---

45. Perhaps I could capture enough of the prohibited assertion with the conditional assertion that if it is true that p, then the man on the street or my earlier self says something true in uttering 'I know that p.'

CHAPTER FOUR

Epistemological Realism

Despite the criticisms of contextualism offered in the previous chapter, I think that there is an important kernel of truth in the view. Contextualism can be thought of as involving two claims, one negative and one positive. The negative claim is that epistemic concepts like knowledge are to an extent indeterminate: the basic structure of these concepts or the sense of epistemic terms like 'know' does not by itself endow propositions involving such terms with determinate truth-conditions, and leaves unsettled whether or not assertions that one does or does not know something are true. The positive claim seeks to alleviate this indeterminacy by positing rules like DeRose's rule of sensitivity to supply assertions involving epistemic terms with determinate truth-conditions in particular contexts. The target of the previous chapter's criticisms was the positive claim; but I think that the negative claim, understood in a certain way, is true and important, and in this chapter I want to suggest how it should be understood and why it should be accepted.

Let us adopt Michael Williams's phrase *epistemological realism* to describe the view that there are facts about what we do and do not know which are independent of and antecedent to our knowledge claims, and which render those claims true or false.[1] If epistemological realism is true, then the conclusions of sceptical arguments are determinately true or false whether we endorse those conclusions or reject them as absurd. Contextualism rejects an absolute form of epistemological realism since it maintains that a given knowledge claim can be true in one context and false in another; but it is compatible with a version of epistemological re-

---

Much of the material in this chapter is a revised and expanded version of parts of "Realism and the Scope of Knowledge," *Pacific Philosophical Quarterly* 64 (1983), 281–296.

1. Williams, *Unnatural Doubts*, 87–134.

alism that relativizes facts about knowledge to a context. The conceptions of knowledge and epistemic possibility I began sketching in Chapter 2 represent another form a rejection of epistemological realism might take, for on that account the truth of claims about knowledge and possibility is constituted in part by our acceptance of those claims, and there are thus no facts antecedent to and independent of those claims which render them true or false.

In this chapter I want to continue developing this account of knowledge and possibility. I'll begin by discussing the connection between epistemological realism and the treatment of scepticism offered in this book. Then I will propose an account of the communicative role of terms like 'know' that parallels a familiar account of the communicative role of the term 'true' and that supports a rejection of epistemological realism. Next I'll offer a semantics for the proposed treatment of knowledge and possibility based on the topological concepts of interior and closure, a semantics that demonstrates the coherence of a nonrealist account of epistemic concepts. And finally in an appendix I'll use this semantics to try to resolve some issues concerning the broader debate over realism about truth.

1. Epistemological Realism and Sceptical Arguments

The history of philosophy is replete with disputes over various views for which the term 'realism' seems appropriate. While the term suggests that such disputes are fundamentally ontological in nature, Michael Dummett and others have sought to characterize realism in terms of the relation between truth and acceptance.[2] Consider the propositions constituting a certain area of discourse, propositions to which the notions of truth and falsity are presumed to be applicable, and which we (rationally) accept as true, reject as false, or neither accept nor reject. Realism about that area of discourse holds that the concept of truth applicable to those propositions is strongly independent of our acceptance or rejection of them, in the sense that it is logically or metaphysically possible for those propositions to be true even though we reject them, false even though we accept them, and either true or false even though we neither accept nor reject them. To fully characterize realism in this sense we must specify the

2. See Dummett's writings collected in *Truth and Other Enigmas* (Cambridge, Mass.: Harvard University Press, 1978), as well as his *Elements of Intuitionism* (Oxford: Oxford University Press, 1977), chap. 7, and "What Is a Theory of Meaning? (II)," in *Truth and Meaning*, ed. Gareth Evans and John McDowell (Oxford: Oxford University Press, 1976).

conditions under which our acceptance or rejection of those propositions takes place, with the strongest form of realism being one that makes truth independent of acceptance even under the most stringent conditions— for example, "in the ideal limit of inquiry."[3] Rejections of realism for the area of discourse then take the form of a denial of the independence of truth from acceptance under the appropriate conditions. To draw the contrast in ontological (and perhaps metaphorical) terms, according to realism the propositions are made true or false by facts whose obtaining is logically or metaphysically independent of whether or not we take them to obtain (or whether or not we accept the propositions that say that they obtain); whereas a denial of realism holds that the propositions are made true or false, at least in part, by the fact that we accept or reject them (under the appropriate conditions). Since for most areas of discourse not every proposition belonging to it is one that we either accept or reject (or would accept or reject under the specified conditions), a denial of realism typically involves a rejection of the law of bivalence for the area in question.

Let me enter a few caveats about this characterization of realism. It might be thought that realism about an area of discourse involves an assignment of truth-conditions to its sentences, whereas a rejection of realism amounts to denying that they have truth-conditions or are made true by anything. Against this, Dummett has argued, persuasively I think, that all parties to disputes over realism (should) agree that if a sentence is true, then there must be something in virtue of which it is true.[4] The dispute is over the nature of these truth-makers, with the realist maintaining that they are conditions whose obtaining is independent of our recognition of them or of our acceptance of the sentence as true, and the opponent of realism maintaining that they are recognizable conditions that license our acceptance of it. It is this that leads Dummett to associate a rejection of realism with a rejection of bivalence, since there are bound to be sentences such that neither they nor their negations are made true by recognizable conditions of this sort. Some philosophers have argued against this association of realism with bivalence,[5] but to do so involves a departure from Dummett's characterization of realism, which is the one I am adopting here.

Applied to epistemic propositions containing terms like 'know' and

3. See, for example, Hilary Putnam, "Realism and Reason," in *Meaning and the Moral Sciences* (London: Routledge & Kegan Paul, 1978).
4. See, for example, "What Is a Theory of Meaning?" 89.
5. For example, Simon Blackburn in *Spreading the Word: Groundings in the Philosophy of Language* (Oxford: Oxford University Press, 1984), chaps. 5 and 6.

'possible' (in the epistemic sense), realism then amounts to the view that such claims about knowledge and possibility are true or false independently of our practices of making or denying, accepting or rejecting them. And a rejection of this sort of epistemological realism holds that such claims are made true or false in part by our accepting or rejecting them—"in part" since of course whether or not it is true that, for instance, it is known that p depends also on whether or not it is true that p (whether the truth of p is to be construed realistically or not being in general a separate issue).[6] Though I shall usually use the term 'know' for convenience, what I shall be talking about for the most part is the impersonal notion of knowledge's being available sketched in Chapter 2. It will be recalled that the knowledge that p is available just in case there are relevant practicable ways for members of the relevant community to establish that p. Since what count as "relevant" and "practicable" methods, and what counts as p's being "established," were said to depend on the community's members' assessments, the account of knowledge's being available (and the correlative account of epistemic possibility) offered in Chapter 2 involves a rejection of epistemological realism in the sense just described.

The approach to scepticism offered in this book is based on three points about our attitude toward sceptical arguments and their conclusions. Sceptical arguments, we have seen, are typically arguments having as premises claims that one does not know some sceptical hypothesis to be false (or that the knowledge of its falsity is not available to one), and concluding, via an inference governed by the transmission principle, that one does not know some common-sense proposition, such as that one has teeth, to be true (or that the knowledge of its truth is not available to one). And our attitude toward such arguments, as shown by the durability of scepticism as a philosophical issue, has these elements: first, we accept (on due reflection), or at least are unable to reject in a principled way, the

6. Exactly what is meant by acceptance or rejection here needs, of course, a great deal of qualification and elaboration. As Chapter 2 made clear, I am talking about what members of a relevant *community would* by and large come to accept under certain conditions. This kind of community-wide consensus does, I think, obtain for the kinds of knowledge claims at issue in discussions of scepticism. But of course people within a community often differ in their actual assessment of ordinary knowledge claims, and just how these kinds of disagreements are to be handled is a matter for further discussion (though it may help to alleviate some of these worries to note, as I do in the text, that our concern here is really with the impersonal notion of knowledge's being available sketched in Chapter 2, for which the objects of assessment and acceptance are made clear). My purpose here is not to provide a detailed account of the relation between knowledge, on the one hand, and assessment and agreement on the other, but to offer a theoretical framework that would accommodate such an account.

sceptic's premises; second, our practice of making and assessing ordinary knowledge claims shows that we accept as valid many inferences governed by the transmission principle (the status of which will be considered in the next two chapters), and we often accept certain propositions as known simply *because* they are consequences of other propositions we accept as known; and third, we reject as absurd the sceptic's conclusions. These are descriptive claims about our actual attitudes and practices, claims that, suitably qualified (not everyone of course immediately shares them), I take to be by and large true. What the approach to scepticism offered here adds to them is the claim that these attitudes and practices are perfectly legitimate and acceptable, and that there are no philosophical grounds on which to criticize them or to call for their revision (or to lament our psychological inability to revise them).

But if epistemological realism is true, then these descriptive claims about our attitudes and practices are simply that, descriptive claims about attitudes and practices that are quite independent of the truth and validity of the sceptic's premises and inferences; and moreover, these attitudes and practices *are* subject to criticism and demands for revision. For if epistemological realism is true, we have to say that the sceptic's premises are false (despite our acceptance of or failure to reject them), or that the transmission principle is straightforwardly invalid (since it has invalid instances, namely, sceptical arguments), or that the sceptic's conclusions are true (despite our rejection of them). But then we accept or fail to reject epistemic claims that are in fact false (the sceptic's premises), or we accept as valid inferences that are in fact invalid (the kinds of inferences to be discussed in the next chapter), or we reject epistemic claims that are in fact true (the sceptic's conclusions). And if any of these three apparently exhaustive possibilities obtains, the corresponding practice of accepting or rejecting claims and inferences *ought* to be revised; or if we are unable to revise it our inability to do so ought to be regarded as a manifestation of a fundamental irrationality infecting our epistemic practices.

On the other hand, if epistemological realism is false, the gap between what our attitudes and practices concerning scepticism *are* and what they *ought* to be is erased, and they can be seen as perfectly legitimate. This is clear as far as our attitudes toward the sceptic's premises and conclusions are concerned, for if our acceptance of the former and our rejection of the latter is (part of) what makes the former true and the latter false, then the possibility that those acceptances and rejections are mistaken disappears. The issue of our acceptance of certain inferences governed by the transmission principle as valid is a subtler one, to be taken up in the next two chapters. But as will emerge, it should not be seen as a matter of our accepting inferences governed by a rule of inference that is straightforwardly invalid.[7] Let us now turn to the question whether our notions of knowledge and possibility are to be construed realistically or not.

2. The Communicative Role of Epistemic Terms

What is the point of saying that the knowledge that p is or is not available, that it is or is not possible that p, or that someone does or doesn't know that p? One answer runs along the following lines. Talk about knowledge is talk about a phenomenon that plays a role in the production and explanation of human behavior: Hannibal was able to conquer Rome because the knowledge that he would cross the Alps wasn't available to the Romans; I walk down the hall to the drinking fountain because I am thirsty and know that I can obtain water there. Since we are interested in the explanation of human behavior, it is important that we have terms that refer to a factor that plays such an important role in its production, and in talking about knowledge we simply refer to that factor. Of course, this is compatible with talk about knowledge playing other roles too: to evaluate a person's claims or beliefs, or to endorse or criticize what someone says. But at bottom epistemic discourse is descriptive, and our interest in it stems from our general interest in correctly describing the world.

The trouble with this answer is that it is not at all clear that knowledge *does* play an essential role in the production and explanation of behavior, distinct from the role played by (perhaps sufficiently strong) belief. Can't Hannibal's conquest be equally well explained by the Romans' failure to (correctly) believe that he would come through the Alps? Can't my behavior in walking down the hall to the drinking fountain be explained equally well by my belief that water is to be found there? There may seem to be exceptions to this: perhaps my stubborn persistence in looking for a sock in my dresser drawer despite my prolonged failure to find it is to be explained by the fact that I *know,* rather than simply believe, that it is in the drawer. But it is not obvious that a reference to knowledge is essential here, or that a suitably strong and entrenched notion of belief

7. If we accept epistemological realism, then the kind of conceptual anomaly I am arguing that scepticism represents becomes rather like the straightforward paradox Shiffer argues it presents in "Contextualist Solutions to Scepticism."

would not do as well.[8] In Chapter 2 I suggested that the impersonal notion of knowledge sketched there is compatible with the idea that individual knowledge is a mental state playing a role in the production and explanation of behavior, and can even be used to help flesh out that idea if one finds it plausible to begin with. However, that was not to endorse that conception of individual knowledge, but rather to offer another possible reason to take the impersonal notion of knowledge as basic.

If knowledge is not a causal explanatory notion, what then might be the point of our talk about it? What I want to suggest is that talk about knowledge should be understood in terms of its role in the appraisal of people's assertions: that in saying that something is or isn't known, or is or isn't possible, we are approving of or criticizing things that people say or might say.[9] I shall first lay out the basic idea, and return later to the question whether talk of knowledge might also have a descriptive role.

Let me begin by rehearsing a familiar story concerning the role of the term 'true,' since I want to offer a parallel account of the role of 'know' and its cognates. As F. P. Ramsey pointed out, the term 'true' is redundant in the sense that to assert that a proposition is true is to say just what one would say by asserting the proposition itself.[10] All instances of this schema are thus correct:

(T) It is true that $p \equiv p$[11]

This raises the question why we have the term 'true' in the first place, if calling a proposition true is simply to say what the unadorned proposition says. One answer is that situations can arise in which we wish to endorse or agree with what someone has asserted, even though we are

---

8. Kaplan ("Who Cares What You Know?") has suggested that an alternative explanation of my persistence in looking for the sock is that my initial belief that it is in the drawer is *resilient* with respect to the proposition that I have been looking for it unsuccessfully for fifteen minutes, which means that my initial confidence that it is in the drawer is undiminished by my coming to believe that proposition. Resilience is neither sufficient nor necessary for knowledge.

9. This is perfectly compatible, though, with 'know' also being a term of appraisal of beliefs. See Paul Horwich, *Truth* (Oxford: Basil Blackwell, 1990), 17–18, for the parallel point about 'true.'

10. See Frank Plumpton Ramsey, "Facts and Propositions," in *Philosophical Papers*, ed. D. H. Mellor (Cambridge: Cambridge University Press, 1990).

11. Since I have been treating 'know' as a propositional operator, I have adopted a similar treatment of 'true.' But we could recast the discussion of both in terms of semantic predicates. Actually, in 'It is true that p,' 'true' can be construed as a predicate anyway, as Horwich notes in *Truth*, 17; and so can 'known' in 'It is known that p' and its ilk.

unable to do so by making the same assertion ourselves (perhaps we don't know what he said, but having complete confidence in his veracity, want to endorse whatever it was). We could do this if we were able to assert the infinite disjunction

(1) (He asserted $p_1 \wedge p_1$) $\vee$ (he asserted $p_2 \wedge p_2$) $\vee \ldots$,

incorporating every proposition he could have asserted. Unfortunately, we can't assert an infinite disjunction. But as Stephen Leeds noted,

(2) What he asserted is true

is demonstrably equivalent to (1) just in case the term 'true' conforms to (T), which it does.[12] Indeed, *any* term T that conforms to

(T') $Tp \equiv p$

is such that

(2') What he asserted is T

is demonstrably equivalent to (1). If (T) and (T') both hold, then

(3) It is true that $p \equiv Tp$.

The availability of a term conforming to (T/T') also allows us to object to or disagree with someone's assertion, for given such a term

(4) What he asserted is not true/T

is demonstrably equivalent to

(5) (He asserted $p_1 \wedge \neg p_1$) $\vee$ (he asserted $p_2 \wedge \neg p_2$) $\vee \ldots$

In light of all this, if our language did not already contain the term 'true' conforming to (T), we would be almost bound to introduce a term conforming to (T') allowing us to form propositions equivalent to those containing 'true.'

Two points are worth noting before returning to knowledge. Defla-

12. Stephen Leeds, "Theories of Reference and Truth," *Erkenntnis* 13 (1978), 111–130.

tionism is the view that conformity to (T) is all there is to the concept expressed by 'true,' and that our concept of truth is not a substantive one according to which propositions are made true by the way the world is, as a correspondence theory of truth would have it. Since all parties to disputes over whether or not truth is a substantive notion accept (T)—its obviousness is what recommended it to Tarski as a condition of adequacy on a definition of 'true' in the first place—the foregoing account of the communicative role of the term 'true' and the need for a term playing that role does not by itself serve as an argument for deflationism, since a correspondence theorist could agree that 'true' is perfectly suited to play a communicative role for which we have a need anyway (indeed, Ramsey, who called attention to the redundancy of 'true,' also endorsed a correspondence conception of truth[13]).

The second point to note is that in making legitimate or warranted assertions involving 'true'—'It is true that p,' 'What he asserted is true,' etc.—we must, as with all assertions, be in a position to make them, or satisfy whatever conditions have to be satisfied for us to be entitled to make them, which may include believing them, and having something like reasons, evidence, or justification for them. But in endorsing what someone says by asserting that it is true that p or that what someone asserted is true, we are not *saying* that the conditions that entitle us to make that assertion are satisfied—we are not saying, for instance, that we have a justified belief that p. In general, that the conditions licensing an assertion are satisfied is not part of the content of the assertion, and assertions involving 'true' are no exception to this.

While the need for a term conforming to (T) is clear, the trouble with having such a term alone is that the only negative mode of appraisal it affords ('That's not true') commits us to the negation of the assertion being criticized. What is needed in addition is a device that allows us to register agreement with an assertion but whose negated use allows us to object to an assertion without committing ourselves to its negation. It might be said that in the latter case what we want to object to is the making of the assertion rather than its content, and that we need a device that al-

<hr>

13. See Frank Plumpton Ramsey, *On Truth*, in *Episteme* 19, ed. Nicholas Rescher and Ulrich Majet (Dordrecht: Kluwer, 1991), 11. My own view is that some sort of correspondence conception of truth is correct but that "correspondence" is not a relation between language and the world which can be naturalized. I argue in *Continuity of Wittgenstein's Thought* that Wittgenstein held a similar view, a reading of Wittgenstein also defended by Hilary Putnam in "The Face of Cognition," *Journal of Philosophy* 91 (1994), 510–516. And I think Donald Davidson holds something like this view too: see "The Structure and Content of Truth," *Journal of Philosophy* 87 (1990), 279–328.

lows us to do that. This is certainly a natural way to view the matter, though if we take linguistic *practice* as basic, then it might be argued that the distinction between objecting to the content of an assertion and objecting to the making of it is derivative of the distinction between a mode of objection that commits us to the contrary assertion and one that does not.[14] In any event, it can be seen that a term that conforms to the schema

(K) $Kp \rightarrow p$

(but not conversely) supplies us with such a device, since it can be shown that 'What he asserted is K' implies (1), though 'What he asserted is not K' does not imply (5). In the case of terms conforming to (T'), for any two such terms T and T', $Tp \equiv T'p$, which we might register by saying that any two such terms are coextensive, or that a term's conformity to (T'), together with extralinguistic fact, determines its extension (though in putting it this way I do not mean to imply that the terms have to be treated as predicates). This is not so in the case of terms conforming to (K), which means that a term's conformity to (K) by itself (together with extralinguistic fact) leaves its extension indeterminate.

Finally, there is also a role for a device which enables us to endorse, or at least countenance, an assertion without committing ourselves to it, but which in its negated use allows us to disagree with it. A term conforming to

(P) $p \rightarrow Pp$

(but not conversely) supplies us with such a device, since it can be shown that 'What he asserted is not P' implies (5), though 'What he asserted is P' does not imply (1). As with terms conforming to (K), a term's conformity to (P) by itself (together with extralinguistic fact) leaves its extension indeterminate.

What I want to propose is that 'know,' 'possible,' and their cognates play the roles just described of endorsing and criticizing assertions, that their playing these roles is nearly the whole story about the content of claims involving these terms, and that (K) and (P) represent the only necessary (though of course not sufficient) conditions for the truth of such

14. The idea of treating assertoric practice as primitive and going on to derive assertoric content from it is developed by Robert Brandom in *Making It Explicit* (Cambridge, Mass.: Harvard University Press, 1994) and *Articulating Reasons* (Cambridge, Mass.: Harvard University Press, 2000).

claims.[15] Linguistic evidence makes it clear that propositions involving epistemic locutions can be used to endorse or criticize assertions: 'That's for sure,' 'As we know,' and like expressions typically signal agreement; 'That hasn't been established,' 'We don't know that,' 'That's unproven,' and the like are forms of criticism, as is the stronger 'That's impossible.' 'Perhaps,' 'Possibly,' and 'Maybe' are used to countenance assertions without endorsing them; and 'How do you know?' often serves as the opening gambit in what may turn into a challenge to an assertion. Of course the fact that epistemic locutions like these do play these kinds of roles does not by itself show that they have no additional assertoric content; but it does at least show that playing these roles is part of their raison d'être.

The fact that 'true' conforms to the biconditional (T) allows us to maintain that in asserting that it is true that p one is saying no more than what one says in asserting that p; but 'know' conforms to the conditional (K), and from this alone we cannot draw an analogous conclusion about asserting that it is known that p. To support this further contention I turn first to the diagnosis of Moore's paradox alluded to in Chapter 2, according to which the unassertibility of propositions like 'P, but it isn't known that p,' 'P, but the knowledge that p isn't available,' and similar propositions is to be explained by the fact that the conditions that license the assertion of 'It's known that p,' 'The knowledge that p is available,' and similar factive epistemic propositions coincide with the conditions that license the assertion of p itself.[16] If in asserting that it is known that p one were making a factual claim that went beyond the truth of p, then it would seem that further conditions, beyond those that license the assertion that p, would have to be fulfilled to license this further factual claim. But there are no further conditions that need to be fulfilled in order for one to be in a position to assert that it is known that p. Against this it might be said that there *are* additional truth-conditions for knowledge claims, namely the kinds of belief and justification conditions found in traditional analyses of knowledge—but that these conditions have to be fulfilled in order for it to be assertible both that p and that it is known that p; and thus that while the assertibility-conditions of p and 'It is known that p' coincide, there are necessary conditions for the truth of the latter that are not necessary conditions for the truth of the former. To this I'd reply that this can equally well be seen as an example of the fallacy of incorporat-

15. This will be qualified somewhat in the next section.
16. See *Continuity of Wittgenstein's Thought*, 144–151.

ing the satisfaction of a proposition's assertibility-conditions into its content which I noted in our discussion of the communicative role of the term 'true': for even if one has to believe that p and be justified in that belief in order to be in a position to assert that it is known that p, it does not follow that having a justified belief that p is part of what one asserts in asserting that it is known that p.[17]

The case for the idea that (K) exhausts the necessary conditions for knowledge is strengthened if we accept a proposal Williamson argues for rather persuasively: that the knowledge that p is in fact the condition that licenses the assertion that p, and that to assert what one does not know is to violate the rules governing the making of assertions.[18] For if so, then to challenge an assertion by saying that it is not known to be true or that the knowledge of its truth is not available is to make the *minimal* challenge to the legitimacy of the assertion, one that does not go beyond charging that the minimal condition that must be satisfied in order for the assertion to be legitimate is not satisfied. But our earlier discussion suggested that the minimal challenge to an assertion is the one made possible by the availability of a term conforming to (K) alone (as opposed to the stronger challenge made possible by a term conforming to (T)). If the minimal challenge to an assertion is to deny that it is known, and if this minimal challenge is made possible by a term conforming to (K) alone, then it is plausible to maintain that 'know' conforms to (K) alone.

(It is worth noting that Williamson's proposal is consonant with the idea offered in Chapter 2 that the assertibility-conditions of p and 'I know that p,' 'It is known that p,' or 'The knowledge that p is available' coincide. For if his proposal is correct, the assertibility-conditions for the latter are that it be known that it is known that p, or that the knowledge that the knowledge that p is available be available. But if (see the next section) its being known that p implies that it is known that it is known that p, then it is assertible that p just in case it is assertible that it is known that p. Having said that, I must confess to being torn between Williamson's proposal that the assertibility condition for p is the knowledge that p and my proposal in Chapter 2 that 'I know that p,' 'It is known that p,' 'The knowledge that p is available,' etc., have the same assertibility conditions

17. It might be objected that these remarks apply only to first-person knowledge claims and not to third-person claims. Although this is true, I would argue that if we regard 'know' as expressing the impersonal notion of knowledge's being available, the argument is still cogent.

18. See Williamson, *Knowledge and Its Limits*, chap. 11, for a defense of this view and for replies to the obvious apparent objection that it prohibits false assertions.

as p. I suspect that the intuitions that support the former proposal can be adequately accounted for by the latter proposal, which does not have the seemingly counterintuitive consequence that false propositions are never assertible. The relation between the two proposals depends in part on the acceptability of the principle that knowing implies knowing that one knows, a principle that Williamson rejects but that I find plausible. If we couch that principle in terms of knowledge's being available rather than individual propositional knowledge, its plausibility is enhanced, since it is hard to see how there could be relevant ways for members of the community to establish that p without there being relevant ways for them to establish this. But I shall not try to resolve these issues here.)

A similar case could be made that 'possible,' in the epistemic sense, conforms to (P) alone. But rather than spell it out in detail, let me just recall that we argued in Chapter 2 that 'It is known that p' or 'The knowledge that p is available' and 'It is possible that p' are duals. Hence the case that 'know' conforms to (K) alone amounts to the case that 'possible' conforms to (P) alone. What remains to be seen, though, is whether this conception of knowledge and possibility is coherent. For if there are no conditions independent of our acceptance of epistemic claims sufficient for their truth, how are their truth-conditions to be represented or determined? To answer this I want to sketch a semantics that fits our account of knowledge and possibility.

3. A Semantics for Knowledge and Possibility

Consider a propositional language L with sentences p, q, r, . . . and sentence-forming operators $\vee$, $\wedge$, $\rightarrow$, and $\neg$. An interpretation of L which associates with each sentence p a set of possible situations or states of affairs p which makes it true is an abstract algebra $B_L = \langle \mathbf{B_L}, \cup, \cap, \Rightarrow, \neg \rangle$, where $\mathbf{B_L}$ is a set of subsets of a set X of possible states of affairs, and $\cup, \cap, \Rightarrow$, and $\neg$ are operations on B_L. If the algebra is a Boolean algebra, $\cup, \cap$, and $\neg$ are set-theoretic union, intersection, and complementation, respectively, and $\mathbf{p} \Rightarrow \mathbf{q} = \bar{\mathbf{p}} \cup \mathbf{q}$. Let us assume that the interpretation of L is a Boolean algebra. This is to assume that the interpretation of L is realist in the sense of section 1, for since $\neg \mathbf{p} = \bar{\mathbf{p}}$, either a sentence or its negation is true and bivalence holds. I'll take up the justification of the assumption in the appendix to this chapter.[19]

---

19. For background on the material in this section and the appendix to this chapter, see

Suppose we expand L to L_K by adding a sentential operator K that, intuitively, conforms to (K) and yields sentences Kp that say that the knowledge that p is available. An interpretation of L_K is provided by a *topological Boolean algebra* $\langle \mathbf{B_L}, \cup, \cap, \Rightarrow, ^-, \mathbf{Int} \rangle$, where **Int** is an *interior operation* on the subsets of **X**, that is, an operation (any operation) on subsets of **X** which satisfies the axioms

(I1) $\mathbf{Int}(x \cap y) = \mathbf{Int}(x) \cap \mathbf{Int}(y)$
(I2) $\mathbf{Int}(x) \subseteq x$
(I3) $\mathbf{Int}(\mathbf{Int}(x)) = \mathbf{Int}(x)$
(I4) $\mathbf{Int}(\vee) = \vee$ ($\vee$ being the unit element).

Similarly, if we expand L_K to L_{KP} by adding a sentential operator P that, intuitively, conforms to (P) and yields sentences Pp that say that it is epistemically possible that p, an interpretation of this expanded language is provided by a topological Boolean algebra $\langle \mathbf{B_L}, \cup, \cap, \Rightarrow, ^-, \mathbf{Int}, \mathbf{Cl} \rangle$, where **Cl** is the *closure operation* on subsets of **X**, defined as $\overline{\mathbf{Int}(\bar{x})}$, and thus satisfying

(C1) $\mathbf{Cl}(x \cup y) = \mathbf{Cl}(x) \cup \mathbf{Cl}(y)$
(C2) $x \subseteq \mathbf{Cl}(x)$
(C3) $\mathbf{Cl}(\mathbf{Cl}(x)) = \mathbf{Cl}(x)$
(C4) $\mathbf{Cl}(\wedge) = \wedge$ ($\wedge$ being the zero element).

The interior and closure operations are by definition duals in the sense that

$$\mathbf{Int}(x) = \overline{\mathbf{Cl}(\bar{x})}$$
$$\mathbf{Cl}(x) = \overline{\mathbf{Int}(\bar{x})}.[20]$$

This bears out what I argued in Chapter 2, that knowledge's being available and epistemic possibility are duals, in the sense that it is epistemically possible that p just in case the knowledge that not-p is not available, and vice versa.

In the last section I proposed that the term 'know' be seen as answering the need for a device for endorsing and criticizing assertions which

---

Helena Rasiowa and Roman Sikorski, *The Mathematics of Metamathematics* (Warsaw: Polish Scientific Publishers, 1968), and John Kelly, *General Topology* (New York: Van Nostrand, 1955).

20. Closure and interior are duals by definition; their duality does not follow from the mere fact that they conform to (C1–4) and (I1–4), respectively.

conforms to the schema (K). The operator K's conformity to this schema is reflected in the topological interpretation through the axiom (I2) governing the interior operation. But the three additional axioms mean that this interpretation imputes a structure to the concept of knowledge that goes beyond the conformity of 'know' to (K) alone. But I think that these additional commitments can be seen to be plausible and minor, and should be looked at in perspective. (I1) means that the knowledge of the truth of a conjunction is available just in case the knowledge of both conjuncts is, which is hard to deny. Put in terms of endorsement, it means that one is in a position to endorse a conjunction just in case one is in a position to endorse both conjuncts. (I3) means that the knowledge that p is available just in case the knowledge that the knowledge that p is available is available. This too seems difficult to deny, if we recall that the knowledge that p is available to members of a relevant community just in case there are relevant practicable ways or methods for them to establish that p. For to say that there are *practicable* methods for people in the community to establish that p is to say that there are people in it who have the qualifications, resources, and opportunities to carry them out, and could carry them out if they chose to do so. But if so, it seems hard to deny that there are practicable ways or methods for establishing that there *are* such people, which is all (I3) commits us to. Put in terms of endorsement, (I3) requires that one is in a position to endorse an assertion just in case one is in a position to endorse an endorsement of it. It might be objected that (I3) commits us to the notorious thesis that if one knows something, then one knows that one knows it; and that there are counterexamples to this thesis (for example, the trusting wife might be said to know that her husband is guilty as charged, even though she can't bring herself to admit this, and might be said to fail to know that she knows he's guilty). But first, these alleged counterexamples concern individual or personal knowledge, which is not at issue here. Moreover, I think that the topological interpretation of knowledge can be used to explain away these cases. As will be seen shortly, the topological interpretation allows for looser and stricter notions of knowledge, and most alleged counterexamples to the thesis, it seems to me, involve shifts from a looser to a stricter notion of knowledge (thus when we credit the trusting wife with knowledge of her husband's guilt, we are using a looser notion of knowledge than when we deny that she knows that she knows this).

Perhaps the most problematic axiom governing the interior operation is (I4), which seems to require that the knowledge of necessary truths, or propositions made true by all states of affairs and falsified by none, is always available. This would seem to run counter to recent claims that there are necessary truths knowledge of which is empirical or a posteriori.[21] These claims have not been universally accepted, though, and (I4) at least seems compatible with the traditional Humean view that equates necessary truths with those knowable a priori. Moreover, depending on the expressive powers of the language L, the kinds of propositions that make (I4) problematic might not be formulable.

But I don't think it important that the topological interpretation of knowledge and possibility be reconcilable with every detail of our epistemic claims and practices (for instance, the transmission principle, whose validity some philosophers have denied and whose status will be considered in the next chapter, comes out valid on the topological interpretation). Indeed, part of the overall thesis of this book—that scepticism represents a kind of conceptual anomaly—is that there is no systematic account of epistemic concepts and principles which meshes with every detail of our epistemic practices, and that those practices are none the worse for that. The interest of the topological interpretation is rather that it captures certain fundamental aspects of our epistemic concepts, such as the duality of impersonal knowledge and possibility, and does so in a way that supports a rejection of epistemological realism. Moreover, it shows that the nonrealist conception of knowledge which I have been advocating, on which knowledge claims are ultimately made true or false by our practices of accepting or rejecting them, is a coherent one. And finally, while I have indicated that this interpretation does not mesh with every aspect of our epistemic practices, I do think it comes close to being an intended interpretation of our epistemic discourse, in the sense that notions of knowledge and possibility conforming to it would, I believe, be recognizable as idealizations or variants of our actual epistemic concepts.

How is a topology for a set X to be determined? A topology for X is determined by the open subsets of X, which are those subsets x such that $Int(x) = x$. A topology for X is thus determined by an interior operation on its subsets. How is an interior operation determined? The axioms (I1)–(I4) do not determine a unique interior operation, and it makes no sense to speak of *the* correct topology or interior operation for X. Rather, interior operations are *stipulated*, in the sense that we simply specify a class of subsets of X as a *sub-basis* for a topology, and then by taking intersections and unions of these generate the open subsets and a unique interior

21. See, for example, Kripke, *Naming and Necessity*.

operation for **X**.[22] Put another way, we have to reject what might be called *topological realism*, according to which our choice of a sub-basis and the interior operation determined by that choice either conform or fail to conform to the topological properties **X** possesses independently of that choice. Rather, **X**'s topological properties flow from the subsets we specify as a sub-basis, and there are no grounds on which such a specification can be rejected as incorrect.

A topological interpretation of the language L_K is thus obtained by specifying as a sub-basis subsets of the subsets *p, q, r,* . . . of the possible states of affairs constituting **X** which comprise the truth-conditions of the atomic sentences p, q, r, . . . , and using this sub-basis to generate an interior operation that serves as the interpretation of K. Intuitively, the subsets of *p, q, r,* . . . making up this sub-basis comprise the states of affairs in which the knowledge that p, that q, that r . . . is available, or conditions that license the assertion that p, that q, that r . . . And the important point for our purposes is that what these conditions are is (implicitly) stipulated or fixed by our practices in making and endorsing assertions and knowledge claims. If there is a consensus about the conditions in which certain assertions are permissible and certain knowledge claims are acceptable (as I contend there is in the case of the kinds of assertions and claims relevant to scepticism), then this consensus in practice can be thought of as implicitly determining the interpretation of 'know' and 'possible.' And just as we have to reject the kind of topological realism that would allow a choice of a sub-basis for **X** to be criticized as unfaithful to the genuine topological properties of **X**, so we ought to reject the kind of epistemological realism that would allow that our consensus in practice about which assertions and epistemic claims are permissible or acceptable might fail to be true to the facts about what actually is assertible or known. There are of course constraints on our epistemic claims and practices, and a structure to our epistemic concepts—namely, the constraints and structure imposed by the axioms governing the interior and closure operations, which require our talk about knowledge and possibility to be regulated by such principles as

$$K(p \wedge q) \subseteq Kp \wedge Kq \qquad P(p \vee q) \subseteq Pp \vee Pq$$
$$Kp \rightarrow p \qquad\qquad\qquad p \rightarrow Pp$$
$$Kp \rightarrow KKp \qquad\qquad\quad PPp \rightarrow Pp.$$

22. For details, see Rasiowa and Sikorski, *Mathematics of Metamathematics*, 14–15.

Moreover, our notions of knowledge and possibility are related to the notions of relevant communities, practicable methods of establishing things, and assertibility in the ways discussed earlier. But these constraints and structure leave the extent of knowledge and possibility underdetermined, and what then determines it are our epistemic practices in making, accepting, criticizing, and endorsing assertions and claims about knowledge and possibility. It is conceivable that these practices should have been different than they are, or that they should alter or evolve. It may even be conceivable (though I'm not at all sure) that they should have been so radically different, or should change so drastically, that there should have been or should come to be a consensus that scepticism is correct (while we still employed epistemic terms and concepts). If so, the extent of knowledge and possibility would have been, or would come to be, different than they are. But given our practices as they actually are, there is no room for wondering whether or not those practices are faithful to some underlying epistemic reality, a view that the topological interpretation of knowledge and possibility shows to be a perfectly coherent one.

APPENDIX: REALISM AND THE SCOPE OF KNOWLEDGE

In section 1 I adverted to Dummett's characterization of realism for an area of discourse as the view that the concept of truth for that area's propositions is strongly independent of the concept of rational acceptance, in the sense that it is metaphysically possible for such a proposition to be true or false whether or not we are in a position to accept or assert it, or whether or not we are able to tell or recognize that it is true or false. If the propositions' truth-conditions strongly transcend their assertibility-conditions in this sense, then the law of bivalence applies to them. Realism for an area of discourse can thus be identified with the applicability of the law of bivalence to its propositions.

Dummett has developed a line of argument against realism in this sense.[23] It starts with the assumption that to understand a proposition is to know or grasp its truth-conditions, and then appeals to the principle that this understanding or knowledge must be manifested somehow in speakers' verbal behavior, in the use competent speakers make of it. But what a speaker can manifest in the use she makes of a proposition is her knowledge of its assertibility-conditions, of the conditions that license the

23. See Dummett's works cited in note 2.

proposition's assertion. These conditions must be ones that the speaker is capable of recognizing to obtain, since they govern her use of the proposition. But if the proposition's truth-conditions are realist in the sense of strongly transcending its assertibility-conditions, then they can obtain or fail to obtain whether or not the speaker is able to recognize that they do. But if so, the speaker's knowledge or grasp of what these truth-conditions are could not be manifested in the use she makes of the proposition, since the knowledge she can manifest is limited to her knowledge of its (recognizable) assertibility-conditions. Hence realism must be rejected.

What we make of this argument depends on how we conceive of the relation between truth- and assertibility-conditions. It seems to me that Dummett's argument depends on taking our knowledge of a proposition's assertibility-conditions to be primitive and unproblematic, a knowledge that can in principle be acquired independently of our knowledge of whatever its truth-conditions are. But the conception of assertibility-conditions implicit in the discussion so far is different. A proposition's assertibility-conditions are (in the spirit of Williamson) the circumstances in which the knowledge of its truth is available, and are thus a subset of its truth-conditions. The picture this suggests is that we start with a knowledge of a proposition's truth-conditions, and then determine the conditions under which practicable methods exist for establishing—or, we might just as well say, *recognizing*—that it is true. The knowledge of its assertibility-conditions is thus derived from the knowledge of its truth-conditions, which is reflected in the semantics of the last section by the fact that L_K's propositions' assertibility-conditions are a function of their truth-conditions, the result of applying an interior operation to the subsets of X which constitute their truth-conditions.[24] But on this con-

---

24. This may seem at odds with treating assertoric practice as basic, but in fact I think it is not. Viewing assertibility-conditions as being derived from truth-conditions is part of a theoretical representation of how we conceive of the relation between truth and assertion, one that allows us to see the competent use of language as manifesting a knowledge of its sentences' truth-conditions. It seems to me that Dummett has something like this in mind when he describes "the most sophisticated" response to antirealism as one that "emphasize[s] the *theoretical* character of a theory of meaning. Within such a theory, we explain a speaker's understanding of an expression or a sentence by ascribing to him knowledge of some feature of it or by saying that he associates some semantic element or complex with it; but . . . we do not then need to explain what it is for him to have this knowledge or make this association in terms of his linguistic behavior." Rather, we are attempting to provide "a picture which, taken as a whole, makes sense of a complex phenomenon, that is, makes it surveyable, even though there is no one-one correspondence between the details of the picture and observable features of the phenomenon" (*Elements of Intuitionism*, 377). Dummett does not go on to explore this response.

ception of the relation of truth- to assertibility-conditions, a manifestation of a knowledge of a proposition's assertibility-conditions counts automatically as a manifestation of a knowledge or grasp of its truth-conditions, since the knowledge of the former flows from a knowledge of the latter. Of course, one might reject this conception of the relation of truth- to assertibility-conditions;[25] but it would be question-begging to reject it on the basis of Dummett's argument, since it constitutes an objection to that argument.

This objection, though, does not settle the issue of realism since even if our knowledge of propositions' assertibility-conditions does flow out of our knowledge of their truth-conditions, this does not suffice to establish that those truth-conditions are realist in the sense of making the propositions subject to the law of bivalence. I began the last section by assuming that an interpretation of L was provided by a Boolean algebra, remarking at the time that this was tantamount to assuming a realist interpretation of L. The relation between truth- and assertibility-conditions just sketched leaves open the question whether the proper interpretation of the language under consideration is Boolean or not. But we can use the topological interpretation of knowledge developed in the last section to shed light on the issue of realism in this general sense.

In section 3 we characterized an interpretation of a propositional language L as an abstract algebra $B_L = \langle \mathbf{B_L}, \cup, \cap, \Rightarrow, \neg \rangle$, where $\mathbf{B_L}$ is a set of subsets of a set $\mathbf{X}$ of possible states of affairs, and $\cup, \cap, \Rightarrow$, and $\neg$ are operations on $\mathbf{B_L}$. The interpretation is realist if the algebra is Boolean, in which case $\cup, \cap$, and $\neg$ are set-theoretic union, intersection, and complementation, respectively, and $\Rightarrow = \bar{p} \cup q$. An antirealist interpretation of L associates with each of its sentences the set of its assertibility-conditions, which we are taking to be those states of affairs in which the knowledge of its truth is available. Such an interpretation is an algebra $A_L = \langle \mathbf{A_L}, \cup, \cap, \Rightarrow, \neg \rangle$, in which $\mathbf{A_L}$ is the set of subsets of recognizable states of affairs of $\mathbf{X}$, and $\cup, \cap, \Rightarrow$, and $\neg$ are operations on $\mathbf{A_L}$. But since the negation of a sentence is not in general assertible whenever the sentence itself is not, this algebra will not in general be a Boolean one but rather a *pseudo-Boolean* or *Heyting* algebra, in which $\cup$ and $\cap$ are again union and intersection, but in which $\Rightarrow$ and $\neg$ are defined by the axioms

$$\mathbf{p} \cap (\mathbf{p} \Rightarrow \mathbf{q}) = \mathbf{p} \cap \mathbf{q}$$
$$(\mathbf{p} \Rightarrow \mathbf{q}) \cap \mathbf{q} = \mathbf{q}$$

25. As perhaps Wittgenstein does. See my *Continuity of Wittgenstein's Thought*, 179.

$$(p \Rightarrow q) \cap (p \Rightarrow r) = p \Rightarrow (q \cap r)$$
$$(p \Rightarrow p) \cap q = q$$
$$\neg(p \Rightarrow p) \cup q = q$$
$$p \Rightarrow (\neg(p \Rightarrow p)) = \neg p.$$

Every Boolean algebra is a Heyting algebra. And a Heyting algebra is Boolean if $\neg$ satisfies $p \cup \neg p = \vee$ (or $\neg p = \bar{p}$) for each $p \in A_L$.

There is an important relation between Boolean and Heyting algebras. Given a topological Boolean algebra $\langle \mathbf{B}, \cup, \cap, \rightarrow, \bar{}, \mathbf{Int} \rangle$, let $G(\mathbf{B})$ be the set of its open elements (that is, the sets $\mathbf{b} \in \mathbf{B}$ such that $\mathbf{Int(b)} = \mathbf{b}$), and define $\mathbf{b}_i \Rightarrow \mathbf{b}_j = \mathbf{Int(b}_i \rightarrow \mathbf{b}_j)$ and $\neg \mathbf{b}_i = \mathbf{Int(\bar{b}}_i)$ for all $\mathbf{b}_{i,j} \in \mathbf{B}$. Then $G(\mathbf{B}) = \langle G(\mathbf{B}), \cup, \cap, \Rightarrow, \neg \rangle$ is a Heyting algebra. Moreover, according to a representation theorem due to McKinsey and Tarski,[26] for every Heyting algebra A there exists a topological Boolean algebra B such that $A = G(B)$, and given any Heyting algebra we can construct a topological Boolean algebra that corresponds to it in this way.[27]

The importance of these facts for our purposes is this. We are thinking of speakers as determining the assertibility-conditions of L's sentences by deriving them from their truth-conditions, and doing so by in effect performing an operation on the sets of states of affairs constituting those truth-conditions which has the formal properties of an interior operation. Thus on the "correct" interpretation of L, its sentences' assertibility-conditions are the images under this operation of their truth-conditions. What the representation theorem guarantees is that there is always a realist—that is, Boolean—interpretation of L's sentences which stands in the relation to their assertibility-conditions in which an interpretation must stand if it is to be the correct interpretation of L. Of course it does not follow from this that this realist interpretation *is* the correct interpretation of L. But it does mean that a realist interpretation is always qualified to play this role, and moreover (as we'll see next), under some plausible assumptions about the possible scope of knowledge, uniquely qualified.

Let A_L be the Heyting algebra of L's sentence's assertibility-conditions, and $B_L = \langle \mathbf{B}_L, \cup, \cap, \Rightarrow, \neg \rangle$ be the algebra of L's sentences' actual truth-conditions; and let $\mathbf{K}$ be the operation its speakers can be thought of as performing on them to derive their assertibility-conditions. We have seen that $\mathbf{K}$ has the properties of an interior operation $\mathbf{Int}_L$ on the members of

26. J. C. C. McKinsey and Alfred Tarski, "On Closed Elements in Closure Algebras," *Annals of Mathematics* 47 (1946), 122–162.

27. See Raisowa and Sikorski, *Mathematics of Metamathematics*, 128–130, for details.

$\mathbf{B_L}$. The question now is whether $\mathbf{B_L}$ is a Boolean algebra (and thus $\langle B_L,$ $\mathbf{Int}_L\rangle$ a topological Boolean algebra), and so L's sentence's truth-conditions realist. It is just in case $\neg\mathbf{p} = \bar{\mathbf{p}}$ for each $\mathbf{p} \in \mathbf{B_L}$. But whether or not this is so is not settled by anything so far.

What is needed to settle the question is further information or assumptions about the topological structure of the set of states of affairs comprising L's truth-conditions, which is to say further information or assumptions about the epistemic concepts we attribute to L's speakers. Some of these seem uncontroversial. If we attribute to them a concept of epistemic possibility, corresponding to the closure operation for $\mathbf{Cl}_L$ on members of $\mathbf{B_L}$, and if we assume that it is possible that p in all those circumstances in which the knowledge that not-p is not available, we have $\mathrm{Cl}_L(\mathbf{p}) = \overline{\mathbf{Int}_L(\neg\mathbf{p})}$ for all $\mathbf{p} \in \mathbf{B_L}$. And from this follow

$$\mathrm{Int}_L(\neg\mathbf{p}) = \mathrm{Int}_L(\bar{\mathbf{p}})$$
$$\mathrm{Cl}_L(\neg\mathbf{p}) = \mathrm{Cl}_L(\bar{\mathbf{p}})$$
$$\mathrm{Cl}_L(\mathbf{p} \cup \neg\mathbf{p}) = \vee,$$

for all $\mathbf{p} \in \mathbf{B_L}$.

Now consider the following principle: if it is at least epistemically possible that p, then it is at least epistemically possible that the knowledge that p should become available to us, or if not to us, at least to members of *some* community. This principle can be expressed by

$$(\text{PK*}) \; \mathrm{Cl}_L(\mathbf{p}) = \mathrm{Cl}_L(\mathrm{Int*}(\mathbf{p})),$$

for all $\mathbf{p} \in \mathbf{B_L}$, where $\mathbf{Int}_L{}^*$ is *some* interior operation on $\mathbf{B_L}$, corresponding to *some* concept of knowledge's being available that we might possibly come to possess, or at least members of *some* community might possibly possess or come to possess. And from (PK*) we can derive the realist principle $\neg\mathbf{p} = \bar{\mathbf{p}}$. Given these assumptions, $\langle B_L, \mathbf{Int}_L\rangle$ is a topological Boolean algebra and L's correct interpretation is a realist one. Proof: Substituting $\neg(\mathbf{p} \cup \neg\mathbf{p})$ for $\mathbf{p}$ in (PK*), we have

$$\mathrm{Cl}_L(\neg(\mathbf{p} \cup \neg\mathbf{p})) = \mathrm{Cl}_L(\mathrm{Int}_L{}^*(\neg(\mathbf{p} \cup \neg\mathbf{p}))).$$

But on the left,

$$\mathrm{Cl}_L(\neg(\mathbf{p} \cup \neg\mathbf{p})) = \overline{\mathrm{Int}_L(\mathbf{p} \cup \neg\mathbf{p})}.$$

And on the right,

$$Cl_L(Int_L{}^*(\neg(p \cup \neg p))) = \overline{Int_L(\overline{Int_L{}^*(\neg(p \cup \neg p))})}$$
$$= \overline{Int_L(Int_L{}^*(\overline{p \cup \neg p}))}$$
$$= \overline{Int_L(Cl_L{}^*(p \cup \neg p))}$$
$$= \overline{Int_L(\vee)}$$
$$= \wedge.$$

But if

$$\overline{Int_L(p \cup \neg p)} = \wedge,$$

then

$$Int_L(p \cup \neg p) = \wedge,$$

and so

$$p \cup \neg p = \vee,$$

from which $\neg p = \bar{p}$ follows directly.

It might be objected that to assume, in accordance with (PK*), that the possibility of truth implies the possibility of knowledge or verification is to assume a (weak) form of verificationism, which in a sense is just what is at issue. But I would argue that verificationism, as traditionally conceived in opposition to realism, *restricts* the concept of verification—for example, to the satisfaction of a proposition's observational consequences. The spirit of the present approach to knowledge is just the opposite, for I have been arguing that apart from a few formal constraints, *no* substantive restrictions can be placed on the concept of knowledge or verification. Figuratively, classical verificationism tries to squeeze truth into a fixed notion of knowledge, whereas the present approach allows for the possibility of knowledge's expanding to encompass a fixed notion of truth. As far as I can see, (PK*) even allows for the possibility of verification by an omniscient being, something certainly at odds with verificationism as traditionally conceived.[28]

28. There seem to me to be similarities between the defense of realism just offered and Crispin Wright's conclusion in "Truth as Sort of Epistemic: Putnam's Peregrinations," *Journal of Philosophy* 97 (2000), 335–364, that a "common-sense realism" is vindicated by a principle to the effect that "no genre of states of affairs is essentially beyond our powers of knowledge: under the right—in principle constructively specifiable 'sufficiently good'—circumstances, our powers will 'reach out' to the very facts in question, and opinions formed will be correct" (361).

(PK*) validates the principle

$$(PK^{*\prime})\ Pp \equiv P(K^*(p)).$$

One might worry that this principle runs afoul of the kind of difficulty Frederic Fitch noted involving propositions like p ∧ ¬Kp, of which there are certainly many true examples.[29] Call *strong verificationism* the clearly unacceptable thesis that the knowledge of the truth of every true proposition is available:

$$(SV)\ (p)(p \to Kp).$$

Let *weak verificationism* be the thesis, which some may find plausible, that it is *possible* for the knowledge of every truth to be available:

$$(WV)\ (p)(p \to \Diamond Kp).$$

If we make the uncontroversial assumptions that knowledge is necessarily factive and that it necessarily distributes over conjunction, weak verificationism can be shown to collapse into strong verificationism, since from these assumptions we can derive

$$(1)\ (p)\neg\Diamond K(p \wedge \neg Kp).$$

And if we substitute p ∧ ¬Kp for p in (WV) and combine it with (1), we get (SV). And since (PK*′) might be thought to imply weak verificationism in the sense of (WR), it might be thought to be vulnerable to the same kind of counterexample.

This worry is misplaced. For the kind of possibility operative in (WV), (SV), and (1) is metaphysical possibility whereas in (PK*′) it is epistemic possibility. Consequently (1) has no implications for (PK*′). And this is as it should be, since on reflection (PK*′) can be seen to be perfectly compatible with the obvious fact that there are true propositions the knowledge of whose truth is not available to us. (PK*′) *would* be compromised if it implied, of some particular proposition p, that it is epistemically possible for the knowledge that p is such a proposition to be available to us. But what (PK*′) actually says is that it is possible for the knowledge that

29. Frederic Fitch, "A Logical Analysis of Some Value Concepts," *Journal of Symbolic Logic* 28 (1963), 135–142. I am following Williamson's presentation of Fitch's argument in *Knowledge and Its Limits*, 270–272.

p is such a proposition to be or become available to *someone*—for instance, to the members of a community of superhuman aliens. And there is nothing in the least incoherent in that possibility. It might be replied that (PK*′) *is* compromised by a proposition saying that some particular proposition p is true, but that the knowledge of its truth never has been, is not, and never will be available to anyone. But we can't simply invoke such a proposition to refute (PK*′), since (PK*′) implies that it is epistemically possible that (or loosely, for all we know) there is *no* true proposition the knowledge of whose truth never has been, is not, and never will be available to anyone. It thus appears that (PK*′) and (PK*) are not vulnerable to Fitch-style counterexamples.

The Status of the Transmission Principle

Having considered and rejected in Chapter 3 responses to scepticism that deny the truth of the premises of sceptical arguments, we turn now to the response that denies the validity of the inferences involved in those arguments, inferences governed by the transmission principle. Given what I have suggested about the primacy of practice in establishing the truth of knowledge claims, one might think that this chapter should be extremely brief. For if the kinds of common-sense knowledge claims whose truth the sceptic denies are made true by our general acceptance of them, and if the sceptic's false conclusions are arrived at via the transmission principle from apparently true premises, then must not that principle be straightforwardly invalid?

The situation is not as simple as that, though. To think it is is to think that the validity of the transmission principle (or any rule of inference) is entirely a matter of its brute conformity, or lack of conformity, to practice, and that more indirect considerations concerning it are simply unavailable or irrelevant. But to say that practice is primary in our making and assessing knowledge claims is not to say that our practice is blind: the knowledge claims we make are typically the results of reflection, deliberation, and other forms of ratiocination; and those claims are amenable to explanation and rationalization. What I want to argue in this chapter is that the transmission principle is implicit in our epistemic practices in the sense that it guides our evaluation and criticism of ordinary knowledge claims, and explains why we accept many of the ordinary knowledge claims we do. Moreover, I want to argue, no other principle is available to play the role the transmission principle plays in guiding and explaining our epistemic practices, and so straightforwardly declaring the sceptic's inferences invalid is as much at odds with those practices as is accepting the sceptic's conclusions. Of course, just what we ought to say about the sceptic's arguments and the relations between their inferences and conclusions remains to be seen, and I shall turn to that in the next chapter. My concern in this chapter is with the relation between the transmission principle and ordinary, nonsceptical claims to know, a consideration of which leads to a consideration of the case *for* the validity of the principle (or more accurately, as will become clear, the case *against* declaring the principle *in*valid). There are two broad areas where our epistemic practices seem informed by the transmission principle: the first involves our criticism and rejection of knowledge claims made by others; the second has to do with our acceptance of the idea that knowledge typically can be extended by deduction. I shall look at these areas in turn, and also consider whether a direct case might be made for the validity of the principle. Then I shall consider what sorts of explanations of these practices alternative to the transmission principle might be available, and argue finally that there are none.

1. Principles and Practice

Let me begin by making a prima facie case that the transmission principle is implicit in our epistemic practices in a sense to be explained. Stated in full generality, that principle, it will be recalled, says that knowledge is transmitted by known logical consequence:

(T) $[Kp_1, Kp_2, \ldots, Kp_n, K(p_1, p_2, \ldots, p_n \vdash q)] \vdash Kq.$

And as we saw in the first two chapters, it can also be formulated in terms of epistemic possibility:

(T''') $[K(p_1, p_2, \ldots, p_n \vdash q), P\neg q] \vdash \neg Kp_1 \lor \neg Kp_2 \lor \ldots \lor \neg Kp_n.$

Restricted to a single proposition, (T''') expresses the idea that in order for a proposition to be known to be true, all counterpossibilities to its truth must be ruled out. For ease of exposition I shall usually take K to express individual propositional knowledge, though it should be kept in mind that what it really expresses is the availability of such knowledge, a distinction that will be relevant later when we consider knowledge by deduction.

It is a familiar aspect of our epistemic practice that we generally require people making claims to knowledge to have ruled out counterpossibilities, and are apt to challenge and reject such claims if they have not. If you claim to know that Mary was in the grocery store this morning because you claim to have seen her there, I can challenge your claim by raising the possibility that it was her twin sister, whom I know to be visiting her, that you saw instead. And if you are not able to rule out that possibility, your claim is defeated. The prima facie case for the transmission principle, in the (restricted) form of (T′′′), is that it is implicit in this aspect of our epistemic practice.

What does it mean to say that a principle or rule is implicit in a practice? Some, like Quine, reject the notion altogether, maintaining that unless a convention, principle, or rule has been explicitly adopted, or is explicitly and deliberately being followed, it is meaningless to speak of behavior's being informed by a rule, or of manifesting an implicit adoption of a convention.[1] But Quine himself admits that most would reject this view; and it is difficult to maintain that the kind of epistemic practice just described is "blind," in the sense that the most that can be said about it is that we simply talk that way, and that no explanation of our doing so that appeals to general principles or rules is possible.

But what is the relation between a practice and a principle or rule said to be implicit in that practice? Complete conformity of the practice to the principle is neither necessary nor sufficient for this. That it is not necessary is shown by the competence/performance distinction alone, as well as by an example of Stroud's, to be discussed in a moment, which bears directly on the transmission principle. And that it is not sufficient is illustrated by the so-called sceptical paradox Kripke claims to extract from Wittgenstein, in which a range of behavior conforms to two different rules, only one of which we assume is being followed, or is implicit in that behavior.[2] What I want to suggest is that a principle or rule is implicit in a practice or a form of behavior if it best *explains* that practice or behavior, or figures in the best explanation of it; and that the transmission principle is, in this sense, implicit in the kind of epistemic practice under consideration. Here the practices at issue are the making and accepting or rejecting of knowledge claims, and the transmission explains those

1. W. V. Quine, "Truth by Convention," in *The Ways of Paradox* (New York: Random House, 1966), 98–99.
2. Saul Kripke, *Wittgenstein on Rules and Private Language* (Cambridge, Mass.: Harvard University Press, 1982). Kripke's use of the phrase "sceptical paradox" has misled some into thinking that the problem is an epistemic one. See, for example, G. E. M. Anscombe, "Critical Notice of Kripke," *Canadian Journal of Philosophy* 15 (1985), 103–109.

practices in the sense that we in effect appeal to it in saying why we make, accept, and reject the claims we do.

This might be challenged on the grounds that we do not, in actual practice, require the elimination of all counterpossibilities, but only those that are in some sense "relevant." In Fred Dretske's well-known example, we do not standardly criticize someone's claim to know that the animals before him in the zoo are zebras because he has failed to rule out the possibility that they are painted mules.[3] This indeed shows that our actual epistemic practice doesn't conform exactly to the transmission principle. But it does not, I think, show that that principle is not implicit in our practice in the sense of figuring in the best explanation of it.[4] For consider Stroud's example of the wartime plane spotters.[5] They distinguish between two types of airplanes, Es and Fs, on the basis of their markings. Having observed certain markings on a plane, a spotter says he knows it to be an F, and this claim is accepted by the other spotters and by those to whom they report. But there are other planes, Gs, of which the spotters have not been apprised (perhaps because Gs are rare and of no military significance) which have the same markings as Fs. Because the spotter has not ruled out the possibility that the airplane he takes to be an F is really a G, he does not actually know it to be an F. Yet his claim to know that it is is in accordance with standard plane-spotting practice.

Stroud takes this example to show that one cannot directly appeal, as J. L. Austin does,[6] to our standard practice of making and assessing knowledge claims to demonstrate that the kinds of inferences involved in sceptical arguments are invalid, on the grounds that such arguments require ruling out possibilities we do not normally consider. For it may be that while standard practice is subject to criticism in theory, there are understandable reasons for leaving it unchallenged and unaltered. In the plane-spotting example, the transmission principle explains why the spotters have to rule out the possibility that a plane is an E in order to claim to know it to be an F. It also requires them to rule out the possibility that it is a G before claiming to know it to be an F, but practical considerations override this requirement and we do not hold them to it, even

3. Dretske, "Epistemic Operators."
4. Mark Kaplan, in "Epistemology on Holiday," *Journal of Philosophy* 88 (1991), 132–154, comes close to maintaining that a principle can be implicit in a practice only if the latter exactly conforms to it, a view I find much too confining—for instance, it does not allow for higher-level justifications of principles of the sort we are considering in this chapter.
5. Stroud, *Significance of Philosophical Scepticism*, 67–74. Stroud says that he adapted the example from one of Thompson Clarke's.
6. See also Kaplan, "Epistemology on Holiday."

though their knowledge claims about Fs are literally false. The transmission principle thus both explains their practice of distinguishing Fs from Es (for it requires them to do so), and figures in the explanation of their failure to distinguish Fs from Gs (for its requirement that they do so is overridden by practical considerations).

This receives (what might seem like unexpected) support from Lewis's version of contextualism.[7] Lewis maintains, in effect, that the transmission principle tells us what counterpossibilities to knowledge claims need to be ruled out, but that we then ignore some of these counterpossibilities in ordinary, nonphilosophical contexts. Lewis's contextualism, though, differs from versions like De Rose's, in that he doesn't really supply strict rules or principles specifying how a context determines which counterpossibilities may be legitimately ignored or which are irrelevant.[8] I think that this view, though it might be called a kind of contextualism, is quite close to the one I am advocating here: we rely on the transmission principle to identify the counterpossibilities to knowledge claims that have to be ruled out, but our practice doesn't exactly conform to that principle, since in practice we just ignore some of them; and moreover, we are not to be faulted for this, since it is ultimately practice that determines which of our knowledge claims are actually correct.

But this case that the transmission principle is implicit in our epistemic practices is prima facie only, for we have not shown that some principle alternative to it—for instance, one to the effect that knowledge requires only the ruling out of certain possibilities, or that knowledge is transmitted only to some known consequences but not to others—isn't the one actually implicit in those practices (both in assessing knowledge claims and in countenancing the transmission of knowledge by deductive reasoning), in the sense of best explaining them. This is an open question, to which we shall return.

2. A Direct Case for the Validity of the Transmission Principle

In the next section I shall take up Nozick's attempt to deny the validity of the transmission principle, while still allowing that knowledge may

7. Lewis, "Elusive Knowledge."
8. Lewis formulates a number of rules concerning which possibilities may or may not be ignored, but they are really more in the nature of guidelines. His basic account of knowledge ("Elusive Knowledge," 554) is "S *knows* that P iff S's evidence eliminates every possibility in which not-P—Psst!—except for those possibilities that we are properly ignoring." But Psst! is not a principle. Psst! is a practice.

be transmitted by deduction. But DeRose notes that someone denying its validity in the way Nozick does must be prepared to countenance such "abominable conjunctions" as that while I know that I have hands, I do not know that I am not a bodiless (and handless) brain in a vat.[9] Although there may be ways for a defender of Nozick to defuse the air of absurdity surrounding a conjunction like this, the example suggests that a direct case for the transmission principle's validity might be made by bringing out the absurdity of denying it.

Suppose that one knows (or the knowledge is available) that p is true, and from it one knowingly deduces that q is true (or the knowledge that q follows from p is available), but that, since the transmission principle is invalid, one nevertheless does not know (or the knowledge is not available) that q is true. Let us also adopt a broadly realist view of truth, on which p is made true by the obtaining of certain conditions independent of one's acceptance of p. Then one knows that conditions sufficient for the truth of p obtain, and in knowing that q is a consequence of p, one knows that these conditions are sufficient for the truth of q. So it appears that one knows that conditions sufficient for the truth of q obtain, and yet one does not know that q is true; and surely this is absurd.

The reader may have noticed, though, that this argument—which I'll call the *direct* argument for the transmission principle—is compromised by the fact that it is itself governed by the transmission principle. Spelled out more carefully, the argument goes from two premises

(1) One knows that conditions sufficient for the truth of p obtain.
(2) One knows that if conditions for the truth of p obtain, then conditions sufficient for the truth of q obtain.

to the conclusion

(3) One knows that conditions sufficient for the truth of q obtain.

And this is just an instance of the transmission principle (T). (Moreover, the transition from 'One knows that p is true' to (1) 'One knows that conditions sufficient for the truth of p obtain' might also be taken to involve the principle, as might the transition from 'One knows that q is a consequence of p' to (2).)

We might be tempted to conclude then that the direct argument for the

9. DeRose, "Solving the Skeptical Problem," 28.

validity of the transmission principle is circular or question-begging, since it presupposes the validity of the principle itself. But this would be incorrect: strictly speaking, a circular or question-begging argument (implicitly) assumes as a premise the conclusion it is meant to establish; and as we know from Lewis Carroll's "What the Tortoise Said to Achilles,"[10] the validity of a rule of inference governing an argument cannot, on pain of infinite regress, be included among the argument's premises. Where does this leave the direct argument?

It would be useful at this point to rehearse briefly the dialectic surrounding Hume's argument against justifying rules of inductive inference. Hume divided ways of establishing conclusions into two exhaustive and exclusive categories: by demonstrative reasoning and on the basis of experience. And he further divided the latter category into direct observation and inductive reasoning. He then argued that all inductive arguments are enthymemic, containing a suppressed premise—call it (I)—saying, very roughly, that nature is "uniform," or that the future will "resemble" the past; and hence that inductive reasoning can be justified only if (I) can be justified. But (I) cannot be established by either demonstrative reasoning or direct observation. And since it figures as a premise in all inductive arguments, any attempt to justify it by inductive reasoning would be circular. Hence neither (I) nor inductive reasoning can be justified.

The problem with this argument emerges when we look more carefully into just what the alleged suppressed premise (I) is supposed to say. For Hume it is closely connected to the assumption that nature is governed by unchanging causal laws; but such laws, it turns out, are really licenses to *infer* one event from the occurrence of another.[11] Thus it begins to seem that what (I) really expresses is the acceptability or validity of inductive inference; and if so, the demand that it be treated as a suppressed premise in inductive arguments is, as we know from Carroll, fallacious. This opens the door to what may have seemed like a natural way to justify inductive reasoning in the first place, namely inductively, with past successful applications of inductive reasoning leading us to conclude that it is likely to continue to be successful.[12] It might be objected that such a "self-supporting" justification of induction is ineffective, since inductive

10. Lewis Carroll, "What the Tortoise Said to Achilles," *Mind* 4 (1985), 278–280.

11. David Hume, *An Inquiry Concerning Human Understanding* (New York: Bobbs-Merrill, 1955), 87–89.

12. See, for instance, Max Black, "Self-Supporting Inductive Arguments," *Journal of Philosophy* 55 (1958), 718–725.

reasoning is presumed to be under suspicion.[13] But this objection is misguided, for scepticism about inductive reasoning was an artifact of Hume's original argument, and once that argument is seen to be fallacious, our natural course is to return to our original acquiescence in inductive reasoning, an acquiescence Hume himself acknowledges. All that is needed is what Goodman calls the "constructive task of confirmation theory," which amounts to codifying the valid forms of inductive reasoning by identifying and formulating rules of inductive inference that fit the actual inductive inferences we accept in practice (including any inferences concerning inductive reasoning itself).[14] The barrier to this project, of course, is what Goodman calls the "new riddle of induction," for the rules of inference that strike us as valid have as instances inductive arguments we clearly reject in practice; and we seem unable to modify the rules to achieve the requisite fit between them and our inductive practices.[15]

In the next chapter I shall offer a similar diagnosis of philosophical scepticism, but here I want to apply some of the morals to be drawn from a consideration of the problem of justifying inductive reasoning to the question of the status of the direct argument for the validity of the transmission principle. The main lesson to be drawn is that the fact that the argument is governed by the rule it seeks to motivate does not by itself discredit it. If we found acceptable all applications of the transmission principle, we could perfectly well find the direct argument for it acceptable too. What does render it inefficacious, though, is the analogue of the new riddle of induction: for what philosophical scepticism shows is that there are applications of the transmission principle which we are unwilling—indeed, I am inclined to say, unable—to accept in practice, and so the kind of fit between a rule of inference and its applications needed to justify the rule is not forthcoming. One might be tempted to say of the direct argument that it is either futile or otiose: if the requisite fit between rules and applications is lacking, the argument is futile; but were it forthcoming, and were we to find acceptable all applications of the transmission principle, we would hardly need the direct argument to justify that acceptance.

Nevertheless, I think that the direct argument is a useful heuristic, for it makes vivid and explicit the appeal of the transmission principle. It

13. Dancy, *Introduction to Contemporary Epistemology,* 203.
14. Goodman, *Fact, Fiction, and Forecast,* 66.
15. Ibid., 72–75.

maintains that in knowingly employing a sound application of modus ponens to arrive at q, we establish that conditions sufficient for q's truth must obtain, and thus establish that q must be true, and so at the very least make the knowledge of its truth available. One way to reject this argument is to try to drive a wedge between the truth of a proposition's being established and knowing it, or the knowledge of its truth being available. But given the nature of the latter concept this does not seem tenable—for to establish the truth of a proposition simply *is* to make the knowledge of its truth available, as we saw in Chapter 2. The other way to reject the argument is to deny that we can actually establish in this way that conditions sufficient for q's truth obtain, or that q is true. But to deny this is to deny that knowingly employing a sound application of one of the most basic rules of deductive logic to arrive at a conclusion necessarily establishes that conclusion. And if a knowing and sound application of one of the most basic rules of logic need not actually establish its conclusion, what could? The question sounds rhetorical, but it is not entirely so, for it invites us to consider whether there might be a way of explaining our willingness to countenance knowledge by deduction that does not appeal to the transmission principle in full generality.[16] That is the possibility to which we now turn.

3. Explaining Knowledge by Deduction

The transmission principle provides the simplest and most natural explanation of our willingness to say that we can often extend our knowledge by deriving consequences of what we know, for it maintains that knowledge is always transmitted by known derivations. The most sustained attempt to deny the validity of the transmission principle is Nozick's.[17] On his subjunctive account of knowledge a person S knows that p just in case four conditions are satisfied:

(1) p is true
(2) S believes that p
(3) If p weren't true, S wouldn't believe that p

16. The phrase "knowledge by deduction" is taken from Lawrence H. Powers, "Knowledge by Deduction," *Philosophical Review* 87 (1978), 337–371. Powers's concerns are somewhat orthogonal to ours, as he wants to show that knowledge by deduction is indeed possible, whereas we are taking it as a given, and asking how it is to be explained.

17. Nozick, *Philosophical Explanations*, 167–288.

(4) If p were true in somewhat different circumstances, S would still believe that p.

The subjunctive conditionals (3) and (4) are to be evaluated using Lewis's
possible-worlds semantics for counterfactuals, according to which (3), for
example, is true just in case S does not believe that p in the possible worlds
closest to the actual world in which p is false, while believing it in those
closer worlds in which p is true.[18] This account invalidates the transmission principle, for if p is the proposition that I have hands, the four conditions are presumably satisfied, and I know p to be true; but if q is the
proposition that I am not a handless brain in a vat, condition (3) is not satisfied, since in those worlds in which I *am* a handless brain in a vat, I presumably still believe that I'm not, and so I do not know that q.

Nozick's account of knowledge has come in for a good deal of critical
scrutiny, which I shall not rehearse here. What I want to consider is how,
given that the transmission principle is not valid on his treatment of
knowledge, he proposes to account for the ordinary cases in which we do
regard knowledge as straightforwardly transmitted by known derivability. For an adequate account of knowledge ought to be able to explain the
obvious fact that we typically regard logicians, say, as extending the range
of their knowledge by means of deductive proofs. Less grandly, if I know
that there are ten students enrolled in my seminar and, concerned with
whether a room with a capacity of fourteen will hold them, infer that there
are fewer than fifteen students enrolled, surely I thereby come to know
that there are fewer than fifteen.

Nozick's explanation of why, in cases like this, knowledge *is* transmitted by deduction appeals to his account of what it is to know something
via a certain method. S knows, via a method M, that p just in case

(1') p is true
(2') S believes, via M, that p
(3') If p weren't true, S wouldn't believe, via M, that p
(4') If, in somewhat different circumstances, p were true and S were to
use M to arrive at a belief whether or not p, S would still believe, via
M, that p.[19]

Suppose I know that p and come to believe that q via the following
method M: deductively inferring q from my belief that p (where this of

18. David Lewis, *Counterfactuals* (Cambridge, Mass.: Harvard University Press, 1973).
19. Nozick, *Philosophical Explanations,* 179.

course means inferring q from a proposition I believe to be true, namely p, rather than inferring q from the proposition that I believe that p). In order to know that q it must be the case that if q weren't true, I would not come to believe it via M, by inferring it from my belief that p. And in order for this to be so, Nozick argues, it must be the case that if q weren't true, I would not believe that p (and hence would not infer q from my belief that p). But in a typical case of knowledge by deduction, this condition is satisfied: since p implies q (the proposition that there are ten students in my seminar implies that there are fewer than fifteen), if q were not true (if there were not fewer than fifteen students), p would not be true either (there would not be ten students enrolled); and given the way in which my belief that p is assumed to be subjunctively related to the fact that p (since I am assumed to know that p), if p were not true (if there were not ten students enrolled), I would not believe that p (I would not believe that there were ten); hence if q weren't true (if there weren't fewer than fifteen), I wouldn't believe that p (I wouldn't believe that there were ten), and so would not infer q from my belief that p (I would not infer that there were fewer than fifteen from my belief that there were ten). So I do know, via M, that q (I do know that there are fewer than fifteen students by inferring it from my belief that there are ten). But in sceptical scenarios knowledge fails to be transmitted by deduction, for if p is the proposition that I have hands and q is the proposition that I am not a handless brain in a vat, the third condition is not satisfied; for if I were a handless brain in a vat, I would presumably still infer that I am not by inferring it from my (false) belief that I have hands.[20]

The first thing to note about this explanation is that it is not peculiar to deduction, but exonerates knowledge by any sort of "inference" from p to q as long as, as a matter of nomic necessity, q is true if p is, and the following counterfactual condition is satisfied:

(C) If q weren't true, S wouldn't believe that p (and so wouldn't deduce q from that belief).

Suppose that, as a matter of nomic necessity, there's smoke just in case there's fire. If on this basis I observe smoke and inductively infer the presence of fire, then all the conditions Nozick requires for knowledge by inference are satisfied (in particular, the condition that if there hadn't been fire, I wouldn't have believed there to be smoke). In fact, Nozick's account

20. Ibid., 230–240.

doesn't even require anything that deserves to be called *inference* at all. Suppose that I am unaware of the correlation between smoke and fire but am so "wired" that an observation of smoke simply triggers in me a belief in fire. Then once again, the requisite conditions are satisfied, and I know there to be fire. And this applies to deductive connections as well: if p implies q and my knowledge that p simply triggers the belief that q, then even though I have not *deduced* q from p, I know that q.

Some might see this as a virtue of Nozick's account, for it subsumes knowledge by deduction under a wider category of what, if our intuitions are sufficiently externalist, we might be prepared to call knowledge by inference or transition from one belief to another. But I think that this assessment is untenable. Nozick's account of knowledge is of course a heavily externalist one, and as such has difficulty accommodating the internalist intuition that knowing a proposition to be true often requires one to be cognizant of its evidentiary relations to other propositions. Now I have considerable sympathy for externalism, but one of the reasons for accepting some version of it is that we ought to resist the demand, evident in Hume's argument against justifying induction, to turn all cases of drawing conclusions on the basis of reasons into instances of deductive reasoning by requiring those reasons to be supplemented by additional propositions sufficient to ensure that the conclusion follows logically from those fleshed-out reasons. But the very temptation of this demand suggests that the one case where the internalist intuition is well founded is that of knowledge by deduction, where one comes to know a proposition to be true by becoming aware of its deductive relations to other propositions one knows to be true. For deductive reasoning is what we might call *transparent:* in deducing a proposition from known premises, one sees or realizes that it follows from them (or at least is capable of seeing or realizing this), and so *proves* it, and realizes (or is capable of realizing) that one has proven it (which cannot be said of knowledge by inference in general).[21] This underlies the traditional requirement that proofs be surveyable, that it be possible to follow them or to "take them in," the point of which is to eliminate the possibility that there might be genuine "proofs" which we were incapable of realizing were proofs, and hence which would be useless for actually allowing us to establish their conclusions. This is not to say that whenever one runs through a sound

21. Dummett uses "transparent" in something like this sense in *Truth and Other Enigmas*, 131. Williamson, in *Knowledge and Its Limits*, 95, calls a condition *luminous* if whenever one is in it, one is in a position to know that one is in it, and argues (unconvincingly, to my mind) that no conditions are luminous in this sense.

chain of deductive reasoning one automatically knows it to be sound, for there is always the possibility of mistakes in reasoning which must be guarded against (and we know from Achilles and the Tortoise that we cannot require the proposition that one's reasoning is nonfallacious to figure as a premise in a chain of deductive reasoning). But it *is* to say that when one arrives at a conclusion via a sound chain of deductive reasoning, it ought to be the case that one is capable of realizing that one has thereby proven or established that conclusion, or that the knowledge that one has established it is available to one.

Nozick's account of knowledge by deduction fails to satisfy this requirement, for on it whether one knows the truth of a proposition q arrived at by sound deductive reasoning from a premise p one knows to be true depends on the truth of the counterfactual condition (C), that if q hadn't been true one wouldn't have believed that p (and so wouldn't have deduced q from one's belief that p), which holds for some propositions p and q but not others. It might be thought that we can rectify this deficiency, since it may seem that we can ascertain whether or not (C) holds simply by reflecting on p and q—after all, simple reflection satisfies me that if there hadn't been fewer than fifteen students enrolled in my seminar, I wouldn't have believed that there were ten; while it also satisfies me that even if I were a bodiless brain in a vat I would still believe that I had hands. So why not simply incorporate the outcome of one's reflection on (C) into the reasoning leading from p to q? But if we try to do this we become involved in Achilles and the Tortoise's difficulties (which isn't surprising, since (C)'s role is to guarantee that the deduction of q from p actually establishes q or produces knowledge of its truth). For the original description of the method M by which, on Nozick's original account, I come to know that q is this:

(M) Deducing q from my belief that p.

But to satisfy the demand that the reasoning by which we come by knowledge by deduction be transparent, we have to change the description of the method whereby I come to know that q to something like this:

(M′) Establishing by reflection that if q were false I wouldn't deduce it from my belief that p (since I wouldn't have that belief), and then deducing q from my belief that p.[22]

22. "Then" isn't temporal here, but is merely intended to keep the two mental operations separate.

But now Nozick's account of knowledge via a method requires that if q had been false I wouldn't have come to believe that q via M′; and so transparency requires that I establish this by reflection and incorporate it in my reasoning, which makes the method whereby I come to believe that q something like this:

(M″) Establishing by reflection that if q were false I wouldn't establish by reflection that if q were false I wouldn't deduce it from my belief that p and then deduce it from my belief that p, and then deducing it from my belief that p.

We are thus embarked on a regress, with the successive descriptions of the method supposedly needed to ensure transparency rapidly becoming incomprehensible.

All this is, of course, modulo the assumption that we ought to try to satisfy the internalist demand that knowledge by deduction be arrived at by a transparent method by incorporating the counterfactual condition (C) required to guarantee knowledge by deductive reasoning into the reasoning itself. One might take the moral to be that the fault lies with the internalist demand rather than with applying Nozick's account of coming to know via a method to the case of knowledge by deduction, and that we should simply accommodate our intuitions to any loss of transparency his account entails. But the account is unsatisfactory even if (C) is taken to be an external condition that has to be satisfied for knowledge to be transmitted by deduction. Concentrating on simple or extreme examples encourages the idea that whether or not (C) is satisfied is a relatively clear-cut matter that can be ascertained by reflection—for it seems fairly obvious that if there hadn't been fewer than fifteen students enrolled in my seminar, I wouldn't have believed that there were ten; and that if I were a handless brain in a vat, I would still believe that I had hands. Suppose, though, that I know that (p) I was born in San Diego, and infer that (q) I was born in California (of course this is not really a deductive inference, but since both the transmission principle and the notion of knowledge by deduction are usually intended to cover such analytic entailments, let us treat it as one). Here the counterfactual condition (C) still seems to hold, for if I had been born, say, in Massachusetts, I would most likely not believe I was born in San Diego. But what if I infer that (q) the person I am originated in the solar system, or better yet, in the Milky Way galaxy? Such inferences would seem to be knowledge transmitting (and we can imagine contexts, say a discussion of extraterrestrial life, where they might be germane). But (C) now requires, say, that if the person I am had not originated in the Milky Way galaxy, I would not believe that I was born in San Diego. It is not at all clear that this counterfactual is true, or even how to evaluate it. Perhaps if I had originated outside the Milky Way, the most likely scenario, or at least one to be taken into account, would be that I *would* then be a brain in a vat and believe that I was born in San Diego. Probably the right thing to say is that a counterfactual like this is simply indeterminate. If so, Nozick's account does not validate this case of knowledge by deduction. And the point can be made independently of particular examples. As the consequence q inferred from p becomes weaker and weaker (in the sense that the consequence that I originated in the solar system is weaker than that I was born in California), the inference becomes more and more trivial. But at the same time, the counterfactual (C), if q weren't true S wouldn't believe that p, involves greater and greater departures from actuality, and so becomes harder and harder to evaluate; and the validation of the transmission of knowledge by such inferences thus becomes more and more difficult to accomplish. And it isn't just a question of difficulty, for in the case of some of the weakest consequences, Nozick's account seems to yield the *wrong* answer. Suppose I know that (p) I have hands, and deduce from this that (q) either I have hands or I am not a handless brain in a vat. This consequence of course involves a sceptical hypothesis, but only as a disjunct, and it is hard to see how I could fail to know it to be true. But if q were false, then I would be a handless brain in a vat, in which case I *would* believe that I had hands. So knowledge fails to be transmitted by the inference in question.

Nozick's explanation of knowledge by deduction alternative to the transmission principle does not seem tenable then. It fails to accommodate the transparency of deductive reasoning, and it does not appear possible to rectify this failure. Moreover, it yields no verdict or the wrong verdict concerning many apparent cases of such knowledge.

4. RESTRICTING THE TRANSMISSION PRINCIPLE

Nozick's account of knowledge by deduction can be seen as restricting the transmission principle so that knowledge is transmitted only by those deductions satisfying the counterfactual condition (C). We have seen the shortcomings of that particular account, but what about the general strategy of restricting the transmission principle so that knowledge is transmitted not by *all* known derivations but only by some? Rather than formulate some condition like Nozick's that a known consequence of known propositions must satisfy in order to be itself known, a condition satisfied by "good" consequences but not by the sort of consequences that figure in sceptical arguments, let us consider the possibility of characterizing a restricted notion of derivability such that even though not all propositions known to be derivable from known premises are known to be true, propositions known to be derivable from known premises in this restricted sense are known to be true. An advantage of this strategy is that since this restricted notion is to be a notion of *derivability*, if we can succeed in characterizing it, it could be expected to possess the sort of transparency characteristic of knowledge by deduction. Let us call the proposed restricted notion *epistemic derivability* and write it as $\vdash_e$:

(1) If $p \vdash_e q$, then $p \vdash q$,

though not conversely (for simplicity I shall consider the case of a consequence of a single proposition, though the discussion generalizes easily). Then we could formulate a weaker version of the transmission principle:

(T_e) $[Kp_1, Kp_2, \ldots, Kp_n, K(p_1, p_2, \ldots, p_n \vdash_e q)] \vdash Kq.$

But this strategy seems doomed to fail, for if we impose two plausible conditions on the proposed notion of epistemic derivability, it can be shown to coincide with ordinary derivability, so that every ordinary consequence of a proposition would be an epistemic consequence as well. Let me simply state the conditions first, and speak to their plausibility after showing that they lead to this result. First, assume that if a proposition is demonstrable simpliciter, then it is "epistemically demonstrable":

(E) If $\vdash p$, then $\vdash_e p$.

And second, since epistemic derivability is supposed to be a species of *derivability*, assume that it conforms to modus ponens:

(MP_e) $p, p \supset q \vdash_e q.$

By the deduction theorem

(2) If $p \vdash q$, then $\vdash p \supset q$.

By (E),

    (3) If $\vdash p \supset q$, then $\vdash_e p \supset q$,

and so

    (4) If $p \vdash q$, then $\vdash_e p \supset q$.

But from (MP$_e$),

    (5) If $\vdash_e p \supset q$, then $p \vdash_e q$,

and so from (4) and (5),

    (6) If $p \vdash q$, then $p \vdash_e q$.

But then from (6) and (1),

    (7) $p \vdash_e q$ iff $p \vdash q$.

Thus it does not seem possible to weaken the transmission by introducing a notion of derivability such that the "good" consequences to which knowledge is transmitted are derivable in this sense while the "bad" or sceptical consequences are not.

    This argument depends on the assumptions (E) and (MP$_e$). (E) says that if the truth of a proposition (a logical truth, say) is demonstrable simpliciter, then it is "epistemically demonstrable," in the sense that if one knows (or the knowledge is available) that p is demonstrable, then one knows (or the knowledge is available) that p is true. It might be thought that someone suspicious of the transmission principle in its original form should have qualms about (E) too; but I think such qualms would be misguided. The reason for being suspicious of the transmission principle is that one may think that knowledge can sometimes fail to be transmitted from the premises to the conclusion of a known derivation—for instance, when one's belief in the premises tracks their truth while one's belief in the conclusion does not. But there is no room for such suspicions here, for an ordinary demonstration of a proposition obviously tracks its truth.[23] More generally, the only way to avoid (E) would be (to echo a point made in section 2) by driving a wedge either between demonstrability and es-

23. See Nozick, *Philosophical Explanations*, 186.

tablishment or between establishment and knowledge. But surely to demonstrate the truth of a proposition is to *establish* its truth—if not, what in the world does a demonstration accomplish? And if we have established the truth of a proposition, surely the knowledge of its truth has been made available, for basically that is just what, as we saw in Chapter 2, it means to say that the knowledge of its truth is available. Thus I can see no principled basis for rejecting (E).

What about the assumption (MP_e) that $\vdash_e$ conforms to modus ponens? This might be objected to on the grounds that what we want to rule out are precisely inferences involving modus ponens that lead from a premise like that one has hands to a conclusion like that one is not a handless brain in a vat. That is, of course, part of what we hoped to achieve by introducing a restricted notion of derivability. But the question is whether we can legitimately achieve it by rejecting (MP_e). $\vdash_e$ is supposed to be a notion of *derivability,* and following Gerhard Gentzen we characterize a derivability relation for a language by requiring it to conform to certain rules.[24] One set of rules, which Gentzen called *structural* rules, hold whether the language contains logical constants or not. The other rules, which he called *operational* rules, are introduction and elimination rules for the logical constants the language contains. If the language contains the conditional $\supset$ (as I am assuming that the language under consideration does), there have to be rules of $\supset$-introduction and -elimination; and (MP_e) is simply the rule of $\supset$-elimination.[25]

What about making the conformity of $\vdash_e$ to modus ponens conditional on the fulfillment of some condition (C_e)? We might construe Nozick's strategy along these lines, where the condition is the counterfactual condition (C). Let us abstract from that particular condition, though, and consider the possibility of making epistemic derivability's conformity to modus ponens conditional on *some* condition or other. The problem with this is that we would then have provided not a general elimination rule for $\supset$ but only a partial one, to be applied when the condition, whatever it might be, is satisfied; and so we would not have fully characterized the derivability relation $\vdash_e$.

24. Gerhard Gentzen, "Investigations into Logical Deduction," trans. M. E. Szabo, in *The Collected Papers of Gerhard Gentzen* (Amsterdam: North Holland, 1969), 68–131.

25. Intuitionistic and relevance logics both recognize modus ponens as the rule of conditional-elimination. What relevance logic denies is that the conditional is equivalent to $\neg p \lor q$, for which, it maintains, modus ponens does not hold. See Alan Ross Anderson and Nuel D. Belnap, Jr., *Entailment: The Logic of Relevance and Necessity,* vol. 1 (Princeton: Princeton University Press, 1975), 7, 259.

But another problem with this is that the fulfillment of the proposed condition, whatever it might be, would clearly have to depend on the content of the propositions (substituted for the schematic letters) p and q in (MP$_e$), since what we are trying to do is disallow inferences from premises like that I have hands to conclusions like that I am not a handless brain in a vat, while allowing them from premises like that ten students are enrolled in my seminar to conclusions like that fewer than fifteen are enrolled. But if so we would not really be talking about genuine logical *inference* at all, for (as will be emphasized in the next chapter) logical inferences must be in conformity with rules *all* of whose instances are valid. In the *Tractatus* Wittgenstein maintained that all incompatibility between propositions was truth-table incompatibility, and was a matter of form alone. This did not seem to account for the apparent incompatibility of propositions like 'a is green' and 'a is red,'[26] and in 1929 he attempted to salvage the basic logical framework of the *Tractatus* by introducing, in "Some Remarks on Logical Form,"[27] a new truth-table to be applied to propositions involving attributions of colors and qualities that come in degrees, so as to make the propositions in question truth-table incompatible after all. But he quickly withdrew that paper, probably because he realized that, far from salvaging the logical framework of the *Tractatus*, it basically demolished it, for it made propositions' logical statuses (in this case, which truth-table was to be applied to them) dependent on their subject matter rather than their form.[28] A similar problem attends the suggestion that whether or not a rule of inference like modus ponens can be applied to certain propositions depends on the fulfillment of a condition that depends, in turn, on the content of those propositions. To impose such a condition on the applicability of a rule of inference is to make it not a genuine rule of inference at all. The upshot of this then is that the idea of restricting the transmission principle by introducing a restricted notion of epistemic derivability is not a viable one.

The burden of this chapter has not been to show that the transmission principle *is* valid, but rather to discredit the strategy of defusing sceptical arguments by maintaining that the inferences they involve, inferences

26. In the *Tractatus Logico-Philosophicus* (London: Routledge, 2001) Wittgenstein did not regard color propositions as elementary, but rather implied that analysis would reveal 'a is red' and 'a is green' to be truth-table incompatible after all. But by 1929 he appears to have given up on accounting for their incompatibility in this way.

27. Reprinted in Ludwig Wittgenstein, *Philosophical Occasions*, ed. James Klagge and Alfred Nordman (Indianapolis: Hackett, 1993), 29–35.

28. On Wittgenstein's proposal and its problems, see Dale Jacquette, *Wittgenstein's Thought in Transition* (West Lafayette, Ind.: Purdue University Press, 1998), 160–189.

governed by the transmission principle, are *in*valid. Though we considered an argument *for* the validity of the transmission principle, that argument was inconclusive, and its real effect was to render vivid how closely intertwined that principle is with our use of deductive reasoning. The overall argument has been that the transmission principle is implicit in our epistemic practices, and that those practices evidence our commitment to it, in the sense that it best explains them. In particular, our practices in evaluating knowledge claims are best explained by the principle, even though they do not conform to it exactly. And our practice of countenancing knowledge by deduction evidences an even clearer commitment to it, since the best alternative explanation of it, Nozick's, proves to be unsatisfactory, and it seems impossible to restrict the transmission principle in such a way as to validate legitimate cases of knowledge by deduction while blocking the inferences involved in sceptical arguments. Chapter 3 made the case that the strategy of defusing sceptical arguments by denying their premises is not viable. In this chapter I have tried to show that the strategy of denying the validity of the sceptic's inferences is not viable either.

Appendix: Hawthorne on Knowledge and Lotteries

This book was originally completed before the publication of John Hawthorne's *Knowledge and Lotteries*.[29] Hawthorne's book considers a number of the issues I have been concerned with, and since it has occasioned a great deal of interest and discussion, it seems useful to append a brief account of some of the points of similarity and difference between his treatment of them and my own.

Hawthorne is concerned with the following sort of puzzle. A person confidently asserts something we would ordinarily grant he knows to be true—for instance, that owing to his modest means he will not be able to afford to go on an African safari this year. At the same time, he holds a ticket in a lucrative lottery which on consideration he would admit, and we would agree, he does not know will lose. If his ticket does win, he will be able to afford an African safari, and he is perfectly capable of making this inference. What are we to say about this puzzle—that he does not know that he won't be able to afford a safari, that his knowledge of this

---

29. John Hawthorne, *Knowledge and Lotteries* (Oxford: Oxford University Press, 2004). Page references to this work are placed directly in the text.

is not compromised by his failure to know that his ticket won't lose, that he does know his ticket will lose after all, or something else? Hawthorne's book presents an extremely comprehensive survey of the possible ways of dealing with this kind of puzzle and of the trade-offs they involve.

There is an obvious structural similarity between this puzzle and the one presented by traditional sceptical arguments of the dreaming and demon sort. Both begin with an *ordinary proposition* we take ourselves to know and then introduce a *lottery proposition,* in Hawthorne's case, or one involving a sceptical hypothesis, in the traditional case, which we are inclined to admit we don't know (5 ff). That said, there is an important difference between the lottery puzzle and the traditional one, in that the ordinary propositions our knowledge of which is compromised by our failure to know the lottery proposition—propositions about the future, in the present example—are not ones for which the claim not to know them represents the kind of outrageous affront to common sense that a similar claim about the propositions that I am sitting at a desk or that I have teeth does. Perhaps we *do* speak loosely about our knowledge of the future and similar matters—that is at least a possible view of the matter, whereas I do not think it is a tenable one in the case of traditional scepticism.

Hawthorne is aware of this disanalogy and tries to extend his puzzle to encompass traditional sceptical arguments by introducing lottery propositions concerning, say, my desk drawn from quantum mechanics to the effect that there is a nonzero objective probability that the material inside my desk suddenly unfolds in such a bizarre way that it no longer counts as a desk (4–5). There are problems with this extension, though. Literal lottery propositions represent familiar kinds of propositions that most would readily agree we don't know to be true. The quantum mechanical propositions seem no less contrived and far-fetched than supposedly scientifically based brain-in-a-vat scenarios. Hawthorne offers a nice explanation based on parity of reasoning of why we don't know literal lottery propositions to be true (15–17) which has no obvious application to their quantum mechanical counterparts; and my own inclination is to say that I *do* know that my desk isn't about to suddenly suffer the bizarre fate, despite the nonzero objective probability that it will. In any case, Hawthorne's attempt to extend lottery puzzles to encompass traditional scepticism seems halfhearted, for he rarely alludes to it in the remainder of the book.

Hawthorne's strategy is to assess how various approaches to the puzzle fare with respect to a number of intuitively plausible principles concerning knowledge. Perhaps the most central principle, and the one to which he is most firmly committed, is what is commonly called the *closure principle,* or what I have been calling the transmission principle (in this appendix I shall follow common usage and call it the closure principle), in both single- and multi-premise formulations. Hawthorne treats it as a substantive generalization about knowledge rather than, as I have, a rule of inference. Though the deduction theorem guarantees that we can move back and forth between the two ways of construing it, I explained in Chapter 1 why I think it is preferable to treat it as a rule of inference, and I shall return to this point later. He considers a number of ways of formulating the principle, and his final formulation of single-premise closure is this (34):

Single-Premise Closure (SPC). Necessarily, if S knows *p*, competently deduces *q*, and thereby comes to believe *q*, while retaining knowledge of *p* throughout, then S knows *q*,

with an analogous formulation of *Multi-Premise Closure* (MPC). This version of the principle is more qualified than the one I have been using, but if the principle is formulated in terms of knowledge's being available rather than individual propositional knowledge, the qualifications seem to me to be otiose.

Hawthorne's defense of closure is one I find quite congenial, though in this chapter I have not so much been defending closure as arguing *against* straightforwardly denying its validity (construed as a rule of inference). But this is consonant with Hawthorne's defense of the principle, since apart from noting its role in explaining why we treat knowledge as extendable via deduction (36), something I have also emphasized, he does not offer a positive argument in support of it but rather ingeniously draws out various apparently absurd consequences of denying it.

One strategy for denying closure he considers is to try to restrict its application to what he calls "lightweight" consequences of propositions known to be true, for which knowledge *is* transmitted by deduction, but to deny it for the kind of "heavyweight" consequences that give rise to sceptical conclusions, including the lottery puzzle (42–43). He examines a number of proposals for distinguishing lightweight from heavyweight consequences, arguing quite convincingly that none of them succeed in drawing the proposed distinction in a satisfactory way (43–46). Although these arguments are of a case-by-case sort, the conclusion they are intended to support is consonant with the general argument I offered in section 4 of this chapter to the effect that the principle cannot be restricted in a way that allows knowledge to be transmitted to "good" consequences of known propositions but not to "bad," scepticism-generating ones.

Hawthorne considers three approaches to the puzzle: contextualism, on which the truth of knowledge ascriptions varies with the context or circumstances of the ascriber, and two forms of invariantism, on which they do not (though in one form they may depend on the circumstances of the subject of the ascription). Some of the objections to contextualism I raised in Chapter 3 were directed at the details of the particular version of the view I considered, DeRose's. But there were also more general objections, in particular ones having to do with the difficulty of saying what someone in a less demanding (or just different) context says or thinks in making assertions or expressing thoughts using the word 'know.' Hawthorne's principal objections to contextualism are along these lines (98 ff.), and he develops them in more detail than I did. In particular, he shows that contextualism is incompatible with the following three intuitively plausible principles:

> *True Belief Schema* (TBS). If S believes that *p*, then S's belief is true iff *p*.
> *False Belief Schema* (FBS). If S believes that *p*, then S's belief is false iff not-*p*.
> *Disquotational Schema for 'Knows'* (DSK). If an English speaker E sincerely utters a sentence *s* of the form 'A knows that *p*', and the sentence in the that-clause means that *p* and 'A' is a name or indexical that refers to *a*, then E believes of *a* that *a* knows that *p*, and expresses that belief by *s*.

Moreover, he argues that it is DSK that would have to be given up, and that there is no simple way to modify it to accommodate the alleged context-sensitivity of 'know,' as there is to modify analogous principles for admittedly context-sensitive words like 'local' or 'flat' to accommodate that sensitivity.

The initial objection to contextualism I raised in Chapter 3 was that as a response to scepticism it is a nonstarter, since it assumes that there is a legitimate sense of 'know' on which I don't actually know that I have hands or teeth, an assumption I disputed and traced to a number of fallacies regarding knowledge. Hawthorne makes much the same point (137–140), and for similar reasons, though, oddly, he makes it not in connection with contextualism but rather in connection with what he calls *skeptical invariantism,* an error theory according to which virtually all our ordinary knowledge claims are false. He notes that the idea that there is such an absolute but legitimate sense of 'know' is often motivated (as it is for contextualists) by assimilating 'know' to comparative adjectives like 'flat' or 'empty,' of which we can say that something is (absolutely) flat/empty just in case nothing could be flatter/emptier. "But," he writes, "it is not so clear that we have nearly as secure a grip on what the candidate high standard semantic value for the verb 'knows' is even supposed to be" (138), since there is no clear comparative use of 'know.' He observes that the claim that there is a legitimate "super sense" (139) of 'know' is often based on the assumption that knowledge in this supposedly absolute sense requires the absence of any epistemic counterpossibilities, and that it is always at least *possible* that, say, I have no hands or teeth. But he objects to this reasoning in the same way I did earlier: he in effect treats knowledge and epistemic possibility as duals, so that to say that not-p is possible (for me) is just to say that I do not know that p—which means that we cannot defend the denial of knowledge that p by appealing to some antecedently recognized possibility that not-p (139–140). (Hawthorne's treatment of epistemic possibility differs in one respect from mine, though, for he relativizes it to persons, so that it is possible that p for S at t just in case p is consistent with what S knows at t [26], whereas I have treated epistemic possibility as an impersonal notion, the dual of the impersonal notion of knowledge's being available.)

The final point of contact I want to call attention to is admittedly rather speculative. Throughout most of the book one of the principles Hawthorne uses to assess various approaches to the lottery puzzle is what he calls the Practical Reasoning Constraint (111), which holds that propositions must be known to be true if they are to be employed in practical reasoning. (He usually considers this principle along with the Assertion Constraint [111], which takes knowledge to be the norm of assertion.) But in the last chapter, after trying and failing to characterize a notion of salience that would allow us to say that knowledge requires the absence of salient counterpossibilities, he offers an intriguing suggestion that basically turns the Practical Reasoning Constraint on its head (173 ff.). Instead of appealing to an antecedent notion of knowledge to license the employment of a proposition in practical reasoning, he in effect proposes taking practical reasoning as basic and suggests we take a proposition as known to be true if we regard its employment in practical reasoning as acceptable.

I find this suggestion interesting, though Hawthorne does not develop it in detail. Although I have not spoken at all about practical reasoning, which is what his suggestion concerns, I discussed the link between knowledge (and the term 'know') and assertion in some detail in Chapter 4. Since Hawthorne usually considers the Practical Reasoning Constraint and the Assertion Constraint together, suppose we extend his suggestion to cover assertion too. We might then say that we say that a proposition is known to be true when we regard its assertion as acceptable, and that it is not known to be true when we regard its assertion as unacceptable. This would bring us quite close to the view of Chapter 4 that the root communicative use of 'know' is to enable us to endorse assertions and to object to them without committing ourselves to their negations. This is, as I said, quite speculative, but it seems to me in keeping with Hawthorne's suggestion about practical reasoning and knowledge.

Despite these points of contact, *Knowledge and Lotteries* strikes me in the end as a somewhat frustrating book. Hawthorne considers several accounts of knowledge that provide different approaches to the lottery puzzle and assesses their compatibility or incompatibility with a variety of intuitively plausible principles regarding knowledge, including Single- and Multi-Premise Closure, the Moorean Constraint, the Practical Reasoning Constraint, the Assertion Constraint, the Epistemic Possibility Constraint, the Objective Chance Principle, and the Disquotational Schema for 'knows' (111–112). He treats them all as substantive generalizations about knowledge and declines to offer a relative weighting of their importance (though he views Single-Premise Closure as "pretty much nonnegotiable" [112]). None of the treatments of knowledge he considers is compatible with all of these principles, which leaves us with a broader version of what Shiffer regards as a kind of paradox inherent in our concept of knowledge.[30] There is, however, no attempt to resolve these tensions or conflicts or to diagnose their source. He disavows Noam Chomsky's suggestion that the concept of knowledge may be incoherent (187),[31] but the book ends with a Concluding Parable that suggests that these tensions may well be irresolvable.

What I am trying to do in this book is to offer a particular account of how philosophical scepticism should be diagnosed, what it suggests about the concept of knowledge, and what morals should be drawn from its persistence. I think its significance is not limited to the fact that some principles we find intuitively plausible might have to be revised or abandoned, but is to be found in what it shows about reasoning and argumentation. Whatever the ultimate merits of this treatment of scepticism, it is worth noting that it cannot even be formulated in the framework

30. Shiffer, "Contextualist Solutions to Scepticism."
31. Noam Chomsky, *Rules and Representations* (New York: Columbia University Press, 1980), 82.

Hawthorne provides, since as I argued in Chapter 1 it requires us to construe the closure or transmission principle as a rule of inference rather than as a substantive generalization about knowledge, which is how Hawthorne construes it (as he does all the principles he considers). Let me turn now in the final chapter to a fuller development of that treatment.

Sceptical Arguments and Forms of Reasoning

Having argued in the previous chapters against straightforward refutations of sceptical arguments—either by denying their premises or by deeming the inferences they involve invalid—I want to turn in this last chapter to the question of what the response to these arguments ought to be. The problem, as I see it, is to reconcile the idea that there is nothing "wrong" with sceptical arguments (in the sense that they are not straightforwardly unsound) with the claim that we are nevertheless not to be faulted for rejecting their conclusions, as I take it common sense does. The issues this problem raises concern the relation between *forms* of reasoning and the results of reasoning that we accept in practice, for the very notion of valid reasoning presupposes a certain widespread fit or equilibrium between general forms of reasoning or rules of inference that we find compelling, and particular arguments or inferences that we accept. And what I want to propose is that sceptical arguments represent an instance—somewhat isolated, but nevertheless important—of a failure to achieve this kind of fit between rules and arguments. It is the fact that there is no a priori guarantee that this desired equilibrium will be attained in every area in which we engage in rational deliberation which allows us to maintain that we aren't irrational in rejecting the conclusions of sceptical arguments, and at the same time hold that these arguments aren't straightforwardly defective. Sceptical arguments are, in a sense to be made out, conceptual anomalies.

But the proposal that sceptical arguments are anomalous raises the question whether they represent the only anomalies of this kind. Since the requisite equilibrium between rules and inferences in fact obtains when our deliberations appeal only to the settled areas of logic, why should a slippage between them emerge when we employ rules involving the concept of knowledge? To be convincing, a diagnosis of the problem of scepticism ought not to seem ad hoc, so if the one I am proposing is to be plausible, it ought to be possible to identify some of the features of epistemic discourse that make deliberations involving it conducive to the kinds of anomalies sceptical arguments represent, and it ought to be possible to identify other areas of deliberation which share some of these features and in which we are likely to encounter similar anomalies. To this end, I want to look briefly at other philosophically perplexing issues that may be amenable to a similar diagnosis, ones concerning moral luck and human freedom.

Finally, the approach taken here raises questions about the relation between human agreement in judgments and practices, which seems like a purely contingent matter, and the validity of general patterns of reasoning, which does not; and I shall end with some reflections on agreement, reasoning, and generality.

1. Sceptical Arguments as Anomalous

Despite the risks involved in attempting to speak with the collective voice of common sense, let me try to summarize the set of attitudes I think we come away with from an engagement with philosophical scepticism. Many philosophers will of course not share this assessment; but I think it is far from idiosyncratic, and widespread enough to amount to a kind of datum to be addressed and accounted for. The encounter with scepticism and sceptical arguments begins, typically in an introductory philosophy course, with a concentration on a range of things we, teacher and student alike, take it for granted we know. They may be emblematized by Descartes' example of sitting by the fire or Moore's of having two hands, but we shouldn't lose sight of the fact that the range of these presumed items of knowledge is vast and heterogeneous, and isn't confined to some narrowly circumscribed class of "common sense" beliefs. The next step involves introducing for consideration highly speculative possibilities supposedly incompatible with these particular examples. One's initial reaction to these possibilities is usually to question their comprehensibility, but familiarity with and imaginative elaboration of them usually mitigates these qualms to the extent that it seems legitimate to ask what we should make of them. And it seems hard to say just *what* we should make of them, for while they typically seem, and continue to seem, ridiculous enough to be an embarrassment outside the classroom, we begin to seem uneasy enough about our grasp of the concept of knowledge—which after all is what is at issue—to maintain that we actually *know* that they don't obtain (or at least to maintain this with a vigor commensurate with our conviction that we know the ordinary things we began by focusing on).

At this point our attention is liable to shift to the character of the reasoning that leads from the admission of the outré possibilities to the conclusion that we don't know the many things we take for granted that we do. While this reasoning can be made to seem natural enough, there are enough subtleties about it to warrant considering whether it may nevertheless be fallacious. Notice, though, that the suspicion that the reasoning involved in sceptical arguments is fallacious arises only *after* we have put aside the strategy of dismissing the sceptical possibilities, and results not so much from a suspicion about what the actual fallacy is as from a hunch that since the reasoning takes us from a premise we are reluctant to deny to a conclusion we are loath to accept, it *must* be fallacious. Various proposals may be made concerning the alleged fallacy, some of which may find a degree of acceptance but none of which is likely to command a consensus. And in light of this, we may try to find a way to live with the sceptical conclusion, but to limit its significance by maintaining that it holds only for some artificially strict notion of knowledge of interest only within the confines of the classroom or Hume's study, and of no importance outside such contexts. But in the end this just seems difficult to believe. It is conceded that we don't believe it outside the classroom, and I would maintain that most of us can't really believe it there either. We are left then with a threefold set of attitudes toward sceptical arguments: we are reluctant to reject outright the outré possibilities that figure in their premises; we find ourselves unable to identify in a convincing manner the flaws in their reasoning; and we are unwilling and even unable to accept their conclusions, as we continue to take for granted that we know the things we began by taking for granted we knew.

The problem is that this set of attitudes is liable to strike us as unstable and irrational. Even if we hold, as I think we do, these attitudes toward the premises, inferences, and conclusions of sceptical arguments, we are liable to think that we *ought* not to hold them, and that at least one of them ought to be revised, if we could only figure out which one it is. The reason of course is that we are liable to think that if an argument has true premises and a false conclusion, then it must be straightforwardly invalid; and so unless we are going to reject the argument as invalid, either we ought to be looking for some grounds on which to reject the premises, or we ought to simply accept the conclusion at face value.

What I want to suggest is that this set of attitudes toward philosophical scepticism and sceptical arguments is fine as it is: not only does the foregoing correctly describe a set of widely shared attitudes toward such arguments, but these attitudes are perfectly stable and rational, we aren't to be faulted for having them, and the thought that they ought, at least ideally, to be revised is a misguided one. The idea that there *is* something wrong with them is traceable, as I just noted, to our idea of validity, that is, to the idea that if an argument goes from true premises to a false conclusion it must be straightforwardly invalid. Consequently I take the lessons to be learned from a consideration of scepticism and sceptical arguments to be ones concerning the notions of validity, arguments, inferences, and forms of reasoning.

Impatient readers may have long felt that even raising the issue of the validity of sceptical arguments or the transmission principle is misguided, since the notion of validity is strictly defined for classical first-order logic (which we shall take to be settled logic, the issues involved in the question whether classical logic or some nonclassical alternative should be regarded as "correct" not being germane to the present ones), and sceptical arguments are, in this strict sense, simply invalid. But the definition of validity for first-order logic depends on a clear delineation of its propositions' logical forms and a distinction between its logical and nonlogical vocabulary. Sceptical arguments and the transmission principle are invalid in this sense merely because 'know' is not a logical term (the logical forms of epistemic propositions not being especially problematic); and the issue then is whether we can characterize a well-defined notion of validity applicable to epistemic propositions and sceptical arguments simply by treating 'know' as a logical term. The cogency of both classically valid inferences and inferences like those involved in sceptical arguments was felt (or challenged) long before the codification of the notion of validity applicable to the former in the early twentieth century. And the important questions are whether the conditions that allowed that notion to be codified for classical first-order inferences are also satisfied in ways that allow us to characterize a notion of validity appropriate to the inferences the sceptic invites us to make; and if not, why not?

On the familiar schematic account of validity, a particular argument or inference is valid just in case it is an instance of a valid schema or rule of inference, and an argument schema or rule of inference is valid just in case every argument or inference instantiating it is valid.[1] This sounds circular, but as Goodman puts it, "this circle is a virtuous one."[2] That it is not

---

1. See, for example, W. V. Quine, *Philosophy of Logic* (Englewood Cliffs, N.J.: Prentice-Hall, 1970), 49–51.
2. Goodman, *Fact, Fiction, and Forecast*, 64.

viciously circular emerges when we consider how we might go about delineating the classes of valid schemata or rules of inference and valid arguments or inferences in practice. Let me sketch this in a way that requires comment and qualification, but defer these for a moment. Think of it as a diachronic process in which we begin with a class of actual arguments which in practice we find compelling or which are presumptively valid—call it A_1—and a class of presumptively valid rules of inference R_1 we find intuitively acceptable. Barring divine revelation, there are almost certain to be some arguments in A_1 that don't instantiate a schema or rule in R_1, and schemata or rules in R_1 having instances not contained in A_1. We then try to revise our intuitions about valid rules and inferences in the way Goodman indicates: "A rule is amended if it yields an inference we are unwilling to accept; an inference is rejected if it violates a rule we are unwilling to amend."[3] These revisions result in new classes of arguments and rules A_2 and R_2, and again we are likely to find that there are arguments in the former that don't instantiate a rule in the latter, and rules in the latter instantiated by arguments not in the former. Ideally, the process of mutually revising our argumentative practices and considered intuitions about inferential rules culminates in classes of arguments and rules A_n and R_n which stand in the following sort of equilibrium: *each* argument in A_n is an instance of *some* rule in R_n, and *every* instance of *each* rule in R_n is included in A_n.

This account needs to be viewed in the proper perspective. A diachronic picture of a succession of revisions of classes of rules of inference and arguments is not meant to correspond even roughly to a historically accurate description of how our conception of validity arose and evolved. Rather, it is meant to bring out in a perspicuous way the relations between that conception and the practices and intuitions about reasoning and forms of reasoning on which it depends. In this it resembles the picture of the social contract by which we go from a state of nature to an acceptance of moral principles, or the accounts we find in Quine and Davidson of the enterprises of radical translation and interpretation.[4] None of these purport to be historically or scientifically accurate accounts of anything, but rather are meant to motivate ways of thinking about, and constraints on the content of, moral principles and judgments about meaning and reference.

3. Ibid.
4. See, for example, W. V. Quine, *Word and Object* (Cambridge, Mass.: MIT Press, 1960), chap. 2, and Davidson, "Radical Interpretation," in *Inquiries into Truth and Interpretation.*

It might be objected that even regarded as a heuristic device, this account of what our conception of validity depends on presupposes something like that very concept, since it begins with classes of rules and arguments we find compelling or presumptively valid. The idea behind this objection is that if we are going to portray the concept of validity as dependent in certain ways on practices and intuitions, then the latter ought to be described in neutral behavioral or psychological terms rather than in ways that seem to involve that very concept. Here again, not only is the aim not to give a factually accurate psychogenetic account of the emergence of a certain concept, but I doubt very much that any "neutral" description of the behavioral regularities underlying our conception of validity is even available. Not every transition from sentence to sentence or assertion to assertion counts as an *inference,* and it strikes me as unlikely that we could find some behavioral or psychological correlate of the implicit "hence" or "therefore" that distinguishes the latter transitions. Our account or picture has to be situated within a framework in which we already have a rudimentary conception of a compelling or valid inference (and a rudimentary sense of the forms of sentences or propositions) as one in which an assertion or acceptance of one proposition commits one to an acceptance of another.[5] A diachronic picture is meant to bring out how this rudimentary formal conception of a compelling or valid argument can lead us to a codification of the actual rules governing valid arguments. Relevant comparisons would be with Kantian constructivism, which begins with a conception of moral principles as categorical imperatives and moves to conclusions about the content of those principles; Rawls's attempt to demonstrate how we arrive at particular principles of justice beginning with a conception of rules of justice as the outcome of a fair process of deliberation aimed at finding rules of social cooperation; or Davidson's attempt to show how, beginning with a grasp of a language's syntax, an identification of its sentences, and a grasp of the concept of its speakers' "holding true" those sentences, we arrive at an assignment of references to the language's terms. Even Quine, who purports to appeal only to neutral behavioral facts underlying attributions of meaning to a language's sentences, has to assume an ability to recognize its users' assent and dissent to its sentences, something that already goes beyond a genuinely neutral description of their behavior.

5. For a defense of the idea that a rudimentary conception of inference is already implicit in primitive acts of assertion, see Robert Brandom, *Articulating Reasons* (Cambridge, Mass.: Harvard University Press, 2000), chap. 2.

The fact that a diachronic picture of the codification of the rules of valid inference presupposes practices and intuitions that already manifest a grasp of a rudimentary and formal idea of validity has consequences for how the successive revisions of rules and arguments must go. In particular, our procedure can't be a purely mechanical one along these lines: (1) if R_i contains a rule not all of whose instance are in A_i, then it is to be eliminated from R_{i+1}; (2) if A_i contains arguments that are instances of no rule in R_i, then they are to be eliminated from A_{i+1}. Repeated applications of these two procedures would quickly leave us with few if any valid arguments or rules of inference. Rather, if we find intuitively compelling a rule that validates some arguments we find compelling along with a few we do not, our initial response would not be to drop the rule entirely, but to try to modify it to capture the inferences we are inclined to accept and exclude those we are inclined to reject. And if we find intuitively compelling inferences that do not instantiate rules we are inclined to accept, our first attempt would be to try to formulate new rules that validate those inferences. So not only is a recourse to practices informed by intuitions of validity unavoidable, it is also required if we are to arrive at a substantive codification of valid rules and valid inferences at all.

We are now in a position to see why the schematic account of validity isn't viciously circular. It would be circular—or better, vacuous—if *whatever* inferences or arguments we began with, we were bound to come up with rules of inference that validated them in the way described. But this isn't the case, for there is no guarantee—let alone an a priori guarantee—that the diachronic procedure for codifying the rules of valid inference will actually result in the kind of equilibrium between rules of inferences and actual inferences required to certify both rules and inferences as valid. The procedure by which we attempt to delineate the classes of valid rules of inference and valid arguments involves successive revisions of our practices and considered intuitions. And since it is, in a sense, a contingent matter that these are as they are (though this way of putting it will be discussed further in section 4), it is in a sense a contingent matter whether or not the equilibrium the procedure aims at will be obtained. There is no a priori assurance that there won't continue to be arguments which we simply cannot accept in practice—arguments, say, with premises we regard as true and conclusions we regard as obviously false— which instantiate rules of inference we are unwilling to amend, or which we are unable to revise in ways that invalidate the rejected arguments while continuing to validate other arguments that in practice we accept as compelling. And there is no assurance that we won't continue to accept in practice rules of inference that are instantiated by some arguments we reject. We know of course that for the settled areas of logic, which we are taking to be classical first-order logic, this fit between schemata and arguments is forthcoming. But my contention is that the problem of philosophical scepticism is simply a manifestation of our inability to attain completely the sought-after equilibrium between our argumentative practices and certain forms of reasoning when our reasoning involves the concept of knowledge.

The transmission principle yields as instances sceptical arguments that in practice we can't accept, for while their premises are difficult to deny, their conclusions—that I do not, for example, know that I had parents—are ones we regard as obviously false.[6] Yet although this means that we cannot maintain that the transmission principle is straightforwardly valid, it also seems unacceptable to declare it straightforwardly *invalid* either, for we would then be left without adequate explanations of why claims to knowledge require the ruling out of certain counterpossibilities, and why we routinely regard knowledge as transmitted by known deductions. What we are left with is the threefold set of attitudes toward sceptical arguments I described earlier: we are embarrassed by a flat denial of their premises, we are unable to locate a clear fallacy in the forms of reasoning they exemplify, and we regard their conclusions as obviously false. This set of attitudes would be unstable or objectionable were the requisite equilibrium between rules of inference, including the transmission principle, and arguments governed by them to be forthcoming, for in that case we would have to, or at least we ought to, revise one or more of those attitudes. In the absence of that equilibrium, though, this set of attitudes is neither unstable nor objectionable. It is in this sense that sceptical arguments are anomalous, for in the case of arguments governed by rules drawn from the settled areas of logic, a comparable set of attitudes would indeed be unstable or objectionable.

6. Throughout I have been taking the obvious falsity of the sceptic's conclusions as a given to be accommodated, and have argued at length against denying the truth of the sceptic's premises or the validity of his reasoning. But this seems an appropriate point to note some additional considerations against accepting those conclusions, even in a theoretical spirit (as Wright seems to recommend, and as contextualism does in a different way). On the proposal in Chapter 4 that the role of 'know' is to enable us to endorse or reject an assertion without a rejection committing us to the assertion's negation (as well as on Williamson's proposal that knowing that p is what licenses the assertion that p), accepting the sceptic's conclusions would commit us to the view that we are entitled to assert almost nothing. And unless our inclination is to welcome scepticism as a way station on the road to Pyrrhonian quietism, this seems too high a price to pay.

There is a partial analogy between the anomaly presented by sceptical arguments and Goodman's grue paradox.[7] In the latter a rule of inductive inference—that a generalization is confirmed by its positive instances—that we find intuitively plausible yields as instances both inferences we accept (for example, ones yielding the conclusion that all emeralds are probably green) and inferences yielding conclusions we reject as absurd (that all emeralds are probably grue). The difference, though, is that there are available accounts of inductive inference alternative to the rule that a generalization is confirmed by its positive instances. Goodman himself proposes revising the rule at issue to conform to "projectible" predicates.[8] And there are many other treatments of induction, including best explanation, bootstrapping, and Bayesian accounts, which have motivations independent of the grue paradox, which seem to many to be capable of explaining our inductive practices, and on which the grue paradox arguably does not arise. By contrast, I have tried to show that there is no readily available principle alternative to the transmission principle capable of explaining the epistemic practices the latter appears to govern.

It might be objected that the schematic account of validity is not the only one, and that model-theoretic accounts should be considered too, especially in light of the apparent failure of a schematic account to yield a clear-cut verdict on the validity of sceptical arguments and the rules governing them. On a model-theoretic account a rule of inference is valid just in case all interpretations of the nonlogical terms that make the premises true also make the conclusion true. The schematic and model-theoretic accounts coincide for classical first-order logic,[9] but perhaps they diverge when 'know' is treated as a logical term, in which case precedence might be given to the model-theoretic account.

What makes this untenable is the rejection of epistemological realism. The nonlogical terms in the transmission principle are the schematic propositional letters. The question then is whether all interpretations of or substitutions for them which make the premises true also make the conclusions true (including cases where the conclusions are sceptical ones). According to epistemological realism, knowledge claims are either true or false independently of our acceptance of them, our attitudes toward or intuitions about them, or our practices involving them. If so, then

7. Goodman, *Fact, Fiction, and Forecast*, 72–81.
8. Ibid., 84–122.
9. See Quine, *Philosophy of Logic*, 47–60.

there is a fact of the matter as to whether the transmission principle is truth-preserving under all interpretations. If it is, it is straightforwardly valid; if it is not, it is invalid. If it is valid, then our attitudes toward sceptical arguments stand in need of revision, as they also do if it is invalid. But if we reject epistemological realism, then, as I tried to argue in Chapter 4, whether or not the transmission principle is truth-preserving under all interpretations is underdetermined by the meaning of 'know,' or by the rules governing its application. What determines whether the resulting premises and conclusions are true or false are our practices in accepting or rejecting them, reflected in our considered intuitions about them. But then the model-theoretic account simply reduces to the schematic account, for determining the validity or invalidity of epistemic principles like the transmission principle becomes a matter of looking at how those principles square with our intuitions and practices regarding knowledge claims and the forms of reasoning involving them. For there are no epistemic facts of the matter independent of those practices and intuitions to which the latter can be required to be faithful.

2. CONDITIONS CONDUCIVE TO THE ANOMALY

Why should scepticism and sceptical arguments manifest the kind of anomaly described in the preceding section? It is possible that scepticism is sui generis, and that the anomalous character of sceptical arguments is due entirely to features peculiar to reasoning about knowledge; and certainly the case I have offered so far for this way of looking at scepticism has focused only on issues internal to the sceptical debate. But since the anomaly has to do with the general relations between judgments, inferences, and forms of reasoning, it would be odd if it arose only within the sceptical arena. Moreover, the case for looking at scepticism in this way would be strengthened if we could identify other recalcitrant philosophical issues that could be viewed in a similar fashion. What I want to do now is try to identify some of the general features of scepticism and sceptical arguments that make it possible for the kind of anomaly I have described to arise, and then look for other philosophical problems that share these features.

There are three salient aspects of sceptical arguments: their premises, the inferences they involve, and their conclusions. The first feature is that these conclusions are at odds with judgments or claims about knowledge we are inclined to make prior to and independently of the arguments (call these the contested claims). An important aspect of the sceptical problem is that these contested claims or judgments are ones for which we have some sort of ground or basis that is independent, at least to a degree, of their inferential connections to other claims or judgments. In the case of common-sense claims to knowledge, I have tried to argue that those judgments are grounded in our shared practices; but there are other possibilities, including experiential and intuitive bases. The important thing is that the contested claims can be supported in ways that are to some extent direct.

The second important feature is that the contested claims have inferential ties, via general principles, to other claims or judgments. In the case of sceptical arguments the common-sense claims are related inferentially to judgments about sceptical hypotheses via the transmission principle, but this can be viewed as an instance of a more general pattern, in which the contested claims (for which we have some sort of direct support) involve concepts whose applicability is governed by general rules or principles to which we commit ourselves in making those claims (as the concept of knowledge seems to be governed by the transmission principle, to which we commit ourselves by our practice of making and assessing knowledge claims). It is important that these rules be general ones, with numerous instances or applications, since the kind of anomaly I am trying to diagnose arises only if there are many *un*problematic applications of those principles.

The third feature is that the other claims or judgments inferentially linked to the contested ones via these general principles also admit of an assessment that is independent of those links. In the case of sceptical arguments, the contested knowledge claims are linked inferentially via the transmission principle to claims about our knowledge of the falsity of sceptical hypotheses. But those inferred claims must, it seems, be rejected, since we lack an adequate answer to the question how we know those hypotheses to be false, a question that seems independent of the common-sense knowledge claims. It is because of this that Moore's strategy of inferring our knowledge of the falsity of sceptical hypotheses from our common-sense claims to knowledge seems unsatisfactory. The important thing is that the claims or judgments inferred via general principles from the contested claims should not be ones whose bases are entirely inferential, but ones that can be supported or criticized in ways that are also to some extent direct.

If these three features are exemplified, then the possibility arises that there be a direct case for the contested claims; an implicit case for the general principles that seem to govern the concepts involved in these claims; and a direct case against the claims inferred from the contested ones via these principles. And it is this kind of possibility that the anomaly presented by scepticism represents. But one more thing seems to be required, and that is a rejection of realism for the kinds of claims involved—for if these claims are viewed realistically, true or false independently of our inclination to accept or reject them or of the cases we can muster for or against them, then one or more of the cases for the contested claims, for the general principles, or against the inferred claims must be straightforwardly deficient. And the heart of the kind of anomaly under consideration is that none of them need be.

I should emphasize that not every case of a tension between some common-sense belief and a theoretically motivated conclusion is anomalous in this way. Our experience is arguably of a three-dimensional space and a temporal order in which events in that space have determinate positions. It is difficult if not impossible to imagine an alternative conception of space and time, so much so that Kant thought that it could be shown to hold a priori. Yet this conception conflicts with the conception of spacetime embedded in special and general relativity. But this is not usefully seen as an instance of the kind of anomaly represented by scepticism, for first, the relativistic conception of spacetime isn't inferred from principles implicit in the common-sense one, but rather arises from an effort to account for independent empirical phenomena like the constancy of the speed of light. Second, even if the Kantian conception of space and time is incompatible with the relativistic notion of spacetime, it isn't at all clear that our *experience* (as of) the Kantian conception (which *seems* to support that conception) is incompatible with the relativistic framework and cannot be accounted for within it. And third, since claims about space, time, and spacetime are, I take it, to be interpreted realistically, any genuine incompatibilities between them should presumably be resolved in favor of the relativistic conception, and the common-sense beliefs and the experiences supporting them be rejected as false and illusory.[10]

A more plausible example of a philosophical conundrum that might be viewed in the way I am suggesting is represented by sorites paradoxes, and I think it is no accident that philosophers like Unger and Williamson with a strong interest in scepticism have devoted considerable attention

10. It is interesting in this regard that attempts I have encountered in conversation to defend the common-sense idea of space and time usually involve interpreting relativity theory instrumentally.

to these paradoxes as well.[11] There are certainly similarities between the two problems: in both we start with a claim that seems obvious (e.g., that someone is bald), and then by repeated applications of a principle that seems to govern a concept involved in the initial claim (e.g., that if someone with n hairs is bald, so is someone with n+1 hairs) arrive at an unacceptable conclusion (e.g., that a person with a full head of hair is bald). Nevertheless, I think that the anomaly represented by scepticism is different in character. Sorites paradoxes trade on concepts that are vague or indeterminate, whereas philosophical scepticism is not, it seems to me, traceable to the vagueness or indeterminacy of the concept of knowledge (even granting that it *is* to some extent vague or indeterminate). The contextualist approach to scepticism, one of whose original champions was Unger,[12] is motivated in part by assimilating the concept of knowledge to vague or indeterminate concepts like *bald* or *flat,* and thus by extension seeing sceptical arguments and sorites paradoxes as posing similar conceptual challenges. I have discussed my reasons for being dissatisfied with contextualist approaches to scepticism in Chapter 3, and for those reasons and others I would resist assimilating sceptical anomalies to sorities paradoxes, though I can see why a number of philosophers have been tempted to do so.

Philosophical scepticism presents itself initially as a challenge to our received views about a matter of human concern, the extent of our knowledge of the world. This challenge is unsuccessful, but it is only when the difficulty of accounting for its lack of success in straightforward ways becomes clear that the possibility that it shows something about the nature of reasoning and inference suggests itself. Relativity theory may present a challenge to our received ideas about space and time, but if so the challenge is a successful one. Sorites paradoxes virtually advertise themselves as being about reasoning and inference (it would be ludicrous, for instance, to take them as presenting a serious challenge to the received view that not everyone is bald). It seems to me that philosophical problems that might be illuminated by looking at them in the way I am suggesting we look at scepticism are liable to share its character of challenging received views we hold on matters of importance to us (rather than initially presenting themselves as puzzles about reasoning), challenges we continue to resist without being able to rebut in straightfor-

11. See, for example, Peter Unger, "There Are No Ordinary Things," *Synthèse* 41 (1979), 117–154, and Timothy Williamson, *Vagueness* (London: Routledge, 1994).

12. See, for example, his *Philosophical Relativity* (Minneapolis: University of Minnesota Press, 1984).

ward ways. Two candidates I think worth exploring are the problems concerning the notions of moral luck and human freedom. Unlike philosophical scepticism, in which the role of sceptical *arguments* is so conspicuous, neither of these problems arises as a result of surprising or clever pieces of argumentation, and the role of rules of inference is not as explicit as it is in the sceptical case. Nevertheless, I think there are similarities among the three problems having to do with the relations between the judgments being challenged and the forms of reasoning used to challenge them.

3. MORAL LUCK AND FREEDOM

Let me make it clear at the outset that the discussions of moral luck and freedom in this section are intended as suggestive sketches only. To facilitate the comparison with scepticism I suggest, for instance, that attributions of praiseworthiness, blameworthiness, and spontaneity be construed nonrealistically. Fleshing out these sketches would of course require a defense of these suggestions, which I shall not undertake here.

The problem of moral luck concerns the judgments we make assessing people for actions they have performed. These judgments are constrained by the principle that people should be blamed or credited for actions only to the extent that what they do is under their control (so that, for instance, a person coerced into doing something is not to be blamed for it, at least not as harshly as someone who does the same thing voluntarily). But often what we wind up doing is the result of factors over which we have no control, and yet this fact is typically not reflected in the moral judgments we make of those actions. The distracted driver searching for something decent on the radio who runs over a child who suddenly crosses his path is judged harshly for the negligent killing, whereas another driver, distracted in exactly the same way, but whose path no child suddenly happens to cross, is judged, if at all, only mildly. Yet the portion of what each did which is genuinely under his control seems exactly the same.

The comparison between the problems of moral luck and philosophical scepticism has already been drawn by Thomas Nagel in his well-known essay on the former.[13] Even better for our purposes, the account of scepticism on which he bases the comparison is Thompson Clarke's,

13. Thomas Nagel, "Moral Luck," in *Mortal Questions* (Cambridge: Cambridge University Press, 1979).

an account of which the one offered in this book is a direct descendant.[14] Clarke was, as far as I know, the first philosopher to emphasize the similarities between the kind of reasoning employed in sceptical arguments and the ways of reasoning about knowledge we employ in ordinary, non-sceptical contexts, and to suggest that consequently it is difficult to fault sceptical arguments for obvious fallacies. He leaves open exactly how this reasoning should be characterized and what our response to scepticism and sceptical arguments ought to be, but his approach is clearly of the kind I have tried to develop and defend here.

The assessments at issue are of a person as blame- or praiseworthy for some action he has performed (as opposed to assessments of the situation that results from the action as good or bad). We begin with an agreed-on description of the person's action of the form

(1) S Fs.

The very idea of assessing *persons* for actions they perform presupposes that those actions are under their control, and to the extent that this is not true, the degree to which they may be assessed for the actions is limited. We commonly recognize a range of what Nagel calls "excusing conditions" which indicate an absence of control and which include "involuntary movement, physical force, or ignorance of the circumstances,"[15] among others. Thus someone who betrays a crucial secret as a result of torture or some other form of coercion is absolved (at least to an extent) from moral judgment, as is the person who fails to keep a serious promise because a national emergency grounds all airplane flights just as he is leaving to keep it. (Nor is it only *moral* assessments that are subject to excusing or limiting factors. A person who as a result of arduous research buys a stock that performs exceptionally well is credited with financial sagacity, while the person who buys a winning lottery ticket is not.) The principle that seems operative in ordinary cases like these is something like this:

(2) If S would not have Fed if C had not occurred, and if C's occurrence was something over which S had no control, then S is not subject to assessment for Fing (or at least the extent of such assessment is limited).

14. Thompson Clarke, "The Legacy of Skepticism," *Journal of Philosophy* 69 (1972), 754–769.
15. Nagel, "Moral Luck," 25.

(F*ing* is understood to include both positive and negative actions, like failing to keep a promise.)

Now the problem of moral luck arises because on reflection the range of conditions C which satisfy (2) is much broader than the familiar range of excusing conditions we recognize in practice. The distracted driver would not have committed negligent homicide had the child not veered into his path; the concentration camp guard would not have sent hundreds to their deaths had the Nazis not come to power in Germany; and the rapist would not have committed the act had the victim not suddenly decided to run out to the store late at night. A natural thought is to try to amend (2) to exclude these extended excusing conditions that we don't in fact recognize in practice. But according to Nagel the problem is not a deficiency in (2), which he regards as inherent in very idea of moral assessment:

> The erosion of moral judgement emerges not as the absurd consequence of an over-simple theory, but as a natural consequence of the ordinary idea of moral assessment, when it is applied to a more complete and precise account of the facts. It would therefore be a mistake to argue from the unacceptability of the conclusions to the need for a different account of the conditions of moral responsibility. The view that moral luck is paradoxical is not a *mistake*, ethical or logical, but a perception of one of the ways in which the intuitively acceptable conditions of moral judgement threaten to undermine it all.[16]

The comparison with scepticism is straightforward. We ordinarily regard knowledge claims to be undermined by the failure to exclude certain kinds of counterpossibilities, a principle comparable to the principle (2) governing claims of moral assessment. The sceptic calls our attention to the fact that this principle covers not only the familiar sorts of counterpossibilities we treat in practice as relevant, but also the outré possibilities involved in sceptical arguments, just as "a more complete and precise account of the facts" reveals that the range of excusing conditions satisfying (2) is much broader than the ones we recognize in practice. And just as the principle that knowledge requires the elimination of counterpossibilities is (I have argued) implicit in our epistemic practices and incapable of being restricted in a principled way that eliminates the unwanted possibilities, so (according to Nagel) a principle like (2) is implicit in our practice of moral assessment and cannot be restricted in a princi-

16. Ibid., 27.

pled way to eliminate the problematic kinds of extended excusing conditions that do not in fact affect our practice of moral assessment.[17]

As I said earlier, the role of rules of inference is not as explicit in the problem of moral luck as it is in the case of scepticism; what we have is rather a general principle, (2), governing the assessment of actions satisfying descriptions of the form (1). But in both cases the relevant claims, descriptions, principles, and rules are schematic: we begin with an agreed-on description, F, of the action whose assessment is in question, and then identify conditions C peculiar to that action which satisfy (2).[18] There is no sweeping argument that yields the general conclusion that our practice of moral assessment is illegitimate. Instead, each instance of moral assessment seems undermined by a schematic principle that appears to govern all such instances, together with facts peculiar to that particular case.

But just as our practice of making, assessing, and accepting (some) knowledge claims is not in fact undermined by sceptical arguments, so our practice of moral assessment is not in fact undermined by this general form of argument which seems to show that virtually all actions that are candidates for harsh (or generous) assessment are the result of moral luck; and in practice we persist in our severe judgments of the negligent driver who kills the child, the concentration camp guard, and the rapist. Nor are we wrong to do so,[19] for moral assessments, like epistemic ones, are not, I would claim, to be construed realistically. There are not, I take it, facts about persons and their actions independent of our assessments of them that make it true that someone really is or is not blame- or praiseworthy for something he has done. Rather, people are blame- or praiseworthy for their actions to the extent they are judged to be so, where those judgments are constrained by various principles like (2), but are not answerable to facts independent of the judgments themselves.

The problem of moral luck is, strictly speaking, independent of the problem of human freedom. Even if novel excusing conditions bar our assessment of S for *F*ing, there is still *something* S did which, for all the arguments so far show, he may be assessed; nor do the arguments show that

17. This of course would have to be established. I simply assume it here for the sake of the comparison with scepticism.

18. The proposition that there are no conditions E that, according to (2), bar our assessment of S for *F*ing plays the role of the proposition inferred from the contested one as described in the last section. Our independent basis for rejecting it is a "more complete and precise account of the facts" concerning S's action.

19. Or so I would maintain. Nagel, like Clarke on scepticism, seems somewhat unclear to me about what our response to the problem should be.

this residual action is not one that S did freely.[20] Yet the problem slides into the problem of freedom, for at each stage, as we replace the description of what S did for which he may or may not be held accountable (F'ing) with some more restricted description (F*ing), it still seems possible to identify conditions C* that, according to the schematic principle (2), bar us from assessing S for that action. In the limit then it starts to appear that S performed *no* action for which he may be held accountable. And if we assume that people may, at least sometimes, be held accountable for what they do freely, it starts to appear that there is nothing S did freely.

Let us turn then to the problem of freedom. What I want to do is simply indicate some possible approaches to the problem, framed along broadly Kantian lines, one of which bears similarities to our approach to the problem of scepticism. I shall consider the problem not as one of the freedom of the *will* but rather as one of acting freely, though I shall suggest why we might be tempted to introduce the idea of a free act of will in an attempt to make sense of the idea of acting freely. The problem originates in a certain belief, attitude, or experience we have when we act under what Kant calls "the idea of freedom":

> Now I assert that every being who cannot act except under the idea of freedom is by this alone—from a practical point of view—really free: that is to say, for him all the laws inseparably bound up with freedom are valid just as much as if his will could be pronounced free on grounds valid for theoretical philosophy. . . . Reason must look upon itself as the author of its own principles independently of alien influence. Thus, as practical reason, or as the will of a rational being, it must regard itself as free.[21]

The questions this raises include these: First, what is the propositional content of this "idea of freedom," of this belief, attitude, or experience? Second, how is this idea, belief, attitude, or experience related to other beliefs we may have about ourselves and our actions? And third, is this idea, belief, attitude, or experience correct or veridical (as Kant maintains), or should it be rejected as mistaken or delusory?

It is important that this conception of freedom, whatever its content, is something that we (at least seem to) have a firsthand experience of or at-

20. Indeed, this is part of the dialectic of the problem of moral luck. Even if the distracted driver can't be assessed for negligently killing the child, he presumably *can* be judged for searching through radio stations while driving. The difficulty is that someone who does *merely* that is usually not too harshly assessed.

21. Immanuel Kant, *Groundwork of the Metaphysics of Morals,* trans. H. D. Paton (New York: Harper and Row, 1964), III:4.

titude involving when we regard ourselves and our actions from the first-person standpoint of practical reason. This makes it difficult if not impossible for us to simply reject a belief in it as a mere mistake in light of a "complete and precise account of the facts" about ourselves and the natural order. At the very least some account of the power of the *illusion* of freedom, if that is what we conclude it is, seems required.

Compatibilists introduce the notion of an action's being caused or brought about in a certain way, as a result of a choice, an operative desire, a reflectively endorsed operative desire, or, in general, the satisfaction of some condition on which the performance of the action depends. This notion can be deployed in two ways. It can be held, as compatibilists do, that the idea of freedom under which we act, which we have a firsthand experience of or attitude involving, and which suffices for ascriptions of moral responsibility is this conditional one. Alternatively, it can be held, as Schopenhauer did,[22] that the idea of freedom under which we act, which we *think* we have a firsthand experience of or attitude involving (and which may also be required for ascriptions of moral responsibility) is an unconditional one, but that we are mistaken in believing that we are free in this unconditional sense, and that our apparent experience of or attitude involving it is simply one of or involving an ersatz, conditional kind of freedom.

Kant rejects both of these alternatives. The kind of freedom under whose idea we act "consists . . . in absolute spontaneity," which, whatever else it may involve, is incompatible with what he calls "predeterminism," or with an action's being brought about by or conditional on some temporally antecedent *cause* (though it is consistent with, and indeed requires, that the action be the outcome of the unfettered exercise of practical reason).[23] Moreover, as the passage quoted from the *Groundwork* indicates, he insists that we really *are* free in this unconditional sense, and that our belief in it or experience of it is "valid."

The picture is clouded, though, by the fact that Kant maintains that all natural events are predetermined by temporally antecedent causes, and also says, just before the above quotation from *Religion within the Limits of Reason Alone*, that the problem "is to understand how *predeterminism*, according to which voluntary actions as events have their determining grounds in *antecedent time* . . . can be consistent with freedom, according

22. Arthur Schopenhauer, *Essay on the Freedom of the Will*, trans. Konstantine Kolenda (Indianapolis: Bobbs-Merrill, 1960).
23. Immanuel Kant, *Religion within the Limits of Reason Alone*, trans. T. M. Green and H. H. Hudson (New York: Harper and Row, 1960), 6:49n.

to which the act as well as its opposite must be within the power of the subject at the moment of its taking place."[24] So Kant seems to gesture here toward some form of compatibilism.

Without pretending to make sense of Kant's actual views,[25] suppose we follow him in rejecting conditional accounts of the kind of freedom we take ourselves to have when we act voluntarily as a result of practical deliberation, agreeing that natural events are predetermined in a sense to be indicated, and leaving the compatibility of freedom and predetermination open for the moment. The freedom we take ourselves to have involves "absolute spontaneity," whatever exactly that means, and thus when I regard my acting so as to F from the first-person standpoint of practical reason, I am convinced of the truth of

(3) I F spontaneously.

Let us take it that the occurrence of a natural event E at a time is predetermined just in case its occurrence is derivable from the laws of nature together with a complete description of the state of the world prior to that time (for simplicity I shall omit temporal indices).[26] Since the occurrences of only those events described in the canonical vocabulary of the laws and state description are derivable from them, this leaves open whether *every* natural occurrence O is predetermined. But assuming that we want to avoid a commitment to the type-reduction of all natural events to ones describable in the vocabulary of science, we can capture the idea that every natural occurrence O is predetermined in this way:

(4) If O is a natural occurrence, then O is token-identical with some natural event E whose occurrence is predetermined (in the above sense).

Now the idea of acting spontaneously is murky, but it seems to be governed by the following (schematic) principle:

(5) If an occurrence O is token-identical with some natural event E

24. Ibid.
25. Julius Sensat has pointed out to me that Kant would probably find the treatment of the problem of freedom I am sketching here to be inadequate, since he thought that unless we can show the inference (to be described next) to the conclusion that we never act spontaneously to be flawed in some way, our devotion to the moral law will be undermined.
26. I am assuming for the sake of argument that this familiar characterization of (pre)determinism is tenable, though I think there are problems with it.

whose occurrence is predetermined, then O is not something done spontaneously.

(5) holds, let us take it, for natural occurrences like the falling of a leaf or the eruption of a volcano, most large- and small-scale social events, and most occurrences involving individual persons. It captures the idea that spontaneity, whatever it is, is something we mean to exclude from the natural realm. And it also seems to rule out my acting spontaneously, for if (3) implies

(6) My Fing is a natural occurrence,

and thus by (4) that

(7) My Fing is token-identical with some natural event E which is predetermined,

then it follows from (5) that my Fing is not something I do spontaneously.

What if we want to maintain, though, that the voluntary actions regarded from the first-person standpoint of practical reason *are* done spontaneously? One way, in the spirit of "two worlds" interpretations of Kant, would be to deny (6) and (7) by maintaining that my Fing is *not* a natural occurrence to be token-identified with some predetermined natural occurrence, and thus not a part of the natural order subject to the laws of causality. We might try to bolster this denial by introducing the idea of a free act of *will* from which my action issues, an act which is by its very nature inherently free and which is performed by a locus of agency or noumenal self transcending the natural order and exempt from its laws.[27] This metaphysical detour doesn't help much though, for what seems hard to swallow is the initial idea that my Fing isn't really a natural occurrence (and thus token-identical with some event describable in the canonical vocabulary of science); and positing a free act of will on the part of a transcendental subject from which my Fing issues doesn't seem to make the latter any less an occurrence in the natural world.

The suggestion I want to offer is that we forgo altogether metaphysical strategies for reconciling our commitment to the spontaneity of our actions—(3)—with the idea that they are natural occurrences subject to the

---

27. Rogers Albritton, in "Freedom of Will and Freedom of Action," *Proceedings and Addresses of the American Philosophical Association* 59 (1985), 239–251, has defended the claim that our idea of the will is of something inherently and necessarily free.

laws of nature—(6) and (7)—and just acknowledge that the schematic principle (5) we take to be inherent in our conception of absolute spontaneity and the idea of freedom under which we act has instances we are unable to accept in practice, namely, those in which O is instantiated by voluntary actions regarded from the first-person standpoint of practical reason and which result from the unfettered exercise of that reason. Again, the similarities with our approach to scepticism are clear. We have some judgments we seem unable to give up (concerning the spontaneity of our actions or common-sense claims to knowledge) involving concepts apparently governed by a schematic principle which, if valid, implies propositions we seem to have independent grounds for rejecting (denying the token-identity of our actions with predetermined events or affirming our knowledge of the falsity of sceptical hypotheses), and whose rejection would then be incompatible with the original judgments. But we also seem unable to reject the principle as straightforwardly *invalid* (which would make those rejections compatible with the original judgments) since it seems implicit in judgments to which we are committed. And yet it has instances we are unable to accept.

To sustain the suggestion that the problem of freedom represents an anomaly comparable to the one represented by the problem of scepticism we would need to establish at least three things. First, we would need to show that the idea of freedom under which we act really *is* an unconditional one that can't be captured by conditional analyses, and that the concept of absolute spontaneity involved in it is governed by some principle like (5). Second, we would need to show that we really *are* unable to give up the conviction that when we act as the result of unfettered practical deliberation our actions are free in this unconditional sense. One way might be to argue that the possibility that our sense of freedom and spontaneity might turn out to be a mere illusion makes no sense.[28] Another might be to argue, with Kant, that we can't even engage in deliberative practical reason (as we surely can) unless we take ourselves to be unconditionally free.

The third thing we would need to establish is that the judgments concerning the spontaneity of our actions to which we are committed are not to be construed realistically, as made true or false by some objective feature of our actions which they do or don't possess quite independently of those judgments (for if not, the possibility that those judgments are just straightforwardly mistaken or that the principle (5) inherent in them is

---

28. Arguments to this effect are given by Keith Kaiser in "Being Free and Seeming to Be Free" (unpublished). See also Albritton, "Freedom of Will."

straightforwardly invalid remains open). Here I think the fact that these judgments seem forced upon us when we regard our actions from a certain *perspective,* namely, the first-person perspective from which we regard our actions when we engage in practical reason, may be crucial, for it is tempting to suppose that if "spontaneity" refers to some objective feature of actions, then its apparent presence or absence should not be viewpoint-dependent in this way.[29] I have spoken of our "experience" of our freedom of action in order to register the fact that our sense of it is not a merely theoretical belief subject to refutation by a more precise and comprehensive account of the facts about the world, but rather something that seems forced upon us when we act deliberately. But this talk of experience is misleading if it is taken to suggest an acquaintance with some positive characteristic of our actions which we detect through introspection. What we have when we regard our own actions from the standpoint of practical deliberation is rather a conviction that those actions are spontaneous and free, even while the content of this conviction remains unclear and the compatibility of that freedom with the necessity of the natural order remains indeterminate.

4. Agreement and Generality

In order for pieces of reasoning to be valid, there has to be the kind of equilibrium between our attitudes toward them and toward the forms of reasoning they exemplify which I tried to characterize in section 1. There is, I argued, no guarantee that this kind of equilibrium will be forthcoming in all cases; and I suggested that the problem of philosophical scepticism be seen as representing a failure of it to obtain in the case of certain arguments involving the concept of knowledge. Some might worry, though, that this account of scepticism flirts with a kind of irrationalism. For if there is no guarantee that the fit between arguments we find compelling and rules of inference we accept will always obtain, it must, in some sense, be a contingent matter when it does. But then if the idea of a conclusion's being validly drawn from a set of premises requires agreement among us concerning rules and arguments, and if that agreement is

29. Even if judgments that our actions are free are forced upon us from a first-person point of view, there would still be the question whether this would suffice to ground third-person assessments of freedom and moral responsibility. I am indebted here to Julius Sensat, "Classical German Philosophy and Cohen's Critique of Rawls," *European Journal of Philosophy* 11 (2003), 314–353.

a contingent matter, then we might be tempted to conclude that whether or not the conclusion follows from the premises is a contingent matter too. And surely this can't be correct: for to regard the forms of reasoning we employ when we think and reason as mere patterns of belief formation we happen to find particularly seductive isn't to think of what we are doing when we conform to them as *reasoning* in accordance with them at all. The concept of valid reasoning can't be one whose content varies with the accidents of psychology and sociology, or which depends on regularities of behavior that are subject to alteration. Worries like these, which have been expressed recently by Nagel,[30] are well taken; but I can see no grounds for them in anything I have proposed here, and I want to conclude by addressing some of them, which I hope will also put the approach to scepticism I have offered in this book in clearer perspective.

In the first place it isn't at all clear how the contingent regularities underlying our inferential practices and our conception of validity might be described. I have characterized them as involving a fit or equilibrium between our finding certain inferences compelling and our acceptance of certain rules of inference. But in referring to our attitudes toward *inferences* and rules of *inference* this characterization presupposes that we already possess a conception of the validity of an inference. And if our grasp of the notion of validity presupposes in turn this kind of fit between our attitudes toward inferences and rules, we *do* have an a priori assurance, via a transcendental argument premised on our possession of a conception of valid reasoning, that this equilibrium does by and large obtain. What we do *not* have is an a priori assurance that it holds for any *particular* class of presumptively valid inferences and the rules taken to govern them, which is what opens the door to the account of scepticism I have offered here. Nevertheless, it does seem to rule out the possibility of a world in which we possessed enough of a conception of validity to find certain *inferences* and rules of *inference* compelling, and yet there was virtually no agreement among us concerning the relation between inferences and rules of inference described in section 1. *Given* our grasp of the notion of validity, then, it isn't a contingent matter that this kind of equilibrium by and large obtains.

A comparison with the role played by agreement in Davidson's interpretationist account of meaning and understanding might help.[31] In or-

30. Thomas Nagel, *The Last Word* (New York: Oxford University Press, 1997).
31. See Davidson, "Radical Interpretation" and other writings in *Inquiries into Truth and Interpretation*.

der to understand or interpret the utterances of others we must, according to Davidson, adopt a certain attitude toward them, one that takes them as holding their utterances true, and as agreeing with us by and large in the things they hold true. It might seem like a contingent matter whether we adopt such an attitude toward others or not, and a contingent matter whether they by and large agree with us in their beliefs. But the very content of that attitude presupposes a conception of understanding or interpreting others; and since our possession of that concept presupposes that we adopt that attitude toward (at least some) others and assume that they by and large agree with us, we *do* have an a priori assurance, via a transcendental argument, that others by and large agree with us in their beliefs and, extending the argument to our own case, that most of *our* beliefs are true. What we do not have is an a priori assurance that others agree with us in any *particular* belief, or that any particular belief of ours is true—which is why, as I argued in Chapter 1, this line of reasoning cannot be deployed in an attempt to refute sceptical arguments, which are schematic. But it does mean that given the fact that we do understand and interpret others, it isn't a contingent matter that we regard them as agreeing with us by and large in the things they hold true.

Yet if our possession of the concepts of validity, understanding, and meaning ultimately presupposes agreements in certain attitudes and practices, must there not be psychological and behavioral regularities underlying them whose descriptions and explanations need not involve those very concepts, regularities whose obtaining *is* a genuinely contingent matter? Perhaps so. We might see Quine, for instance, not as establishing the indeterminacy of translation and meaning, but rather as attempting (and failing) to identify the semantically neutral behavioral regularities underlying our conceptions of interpretation and meaning. In the *Investigations* Wittgenstein remarks that a general absence of disputes over whether a rule has been obeyed or not "is part of the framework on which the working of our language is based," and responds to the suggestion that if so then "human agreement decides what is true and what is false" by saying that the kind of agreement in question is not agreement in "opinion" or in "what human beings *say*" but rather "in form of life."[32] For Wittgenstein, forms of life involve shared attitudes, responses, and patterns of behavior, and they are supposed to be conceptually prior to the semantic and psychological concepts they underlie. But notoriously, he never characterizes a form of life in any detail, and I think

32. Wittgenstein, *Philosophical Investigations*, secs. 240–241.

that this is no accident. Even if conceptually neutral patterns of behavior do underlie our conceptual frameworks involving notions like meaning, understanding, validity, inference, and intentional psychological states, it is difficult if not impossible to put the frameworks aside and characterize those patterns in ways that do not presuppose them.

But the worry is ill-founded that if contingent psychological and behavioral regularities, whether readily describable or not, underlie our possession and application of the concepts of validity and inference, then whether or not one proposition may be validly inferred from another is itself a contingent matter. It seems obvious that our possession of *all* concepts has a contingent basis in accidents of our make-up,[33] yet this obvious fact does not in the least threaten the objectivity of those concepts or our application of them. Just as the fact that it is a matter of convention that the words 'cow' and 'animal' mean what they do does not imply that it is a matter of convention that cows are animals, so the fact that our possession of concepts like bachelor, two, four, and addition depends on contingent aspects of our nature does not mean that it is not a necessary truth that bachelors are unmarried or that two plus two equals four. To think otherwise is to confuse the conditions for the possession of a concept with the conditions for its application. Even if we accept a Davidsonian argument to the effect that we can possess certain concepts only if it can be known a priori that we are mostly correct in their applications, it does not follow that any of those concepts can be known a priori to apply in any particular instances. In the case of validity and inference, our possession of those concepts requires a certain stable pattern in our application of them, but even if our applying them in that way is in some sense a contingent matter, or is underlain by contingent psychological and behavioral regularities, it simply does not follow that whether the conclusion of an argument validly follows from its premises is a contingent matter dependent on accidents of our individual and social natures. The pattern of our application of these concepts does indeed have the stability required to make our judgments concerning validity perfectly objective and necessary (when correct) in the overwhelming number of cases in which we are in a position to make them. This pattern is not perfect, though: in the case of scepticism (and perhaps some other philosophical problems), it is unstable enough to render the arguments for it neither straightfor-

---

33. In the *Tractatus* Wittgenstein maintains that whether a proposition had a sense could not depend on any contingent fact (2.0211–2.0212). But in the *Investigations* (II, xii) he maintains that our possession of the concepts we have depends on "certain very general facts of nature."

wardly valid nor invalid, which leaves it open to us to reject, as we certainly do, their conclusions without identifying particular flaws in the reasoning they contain.

But if nothing in our approach to scepticism calls the objectivity of reasoning into question, it does raise questions about what might be termed its generality. Our practice of reasoning is regulated by a certain ideal that Nagel describes in this way:

> The essential characteristic of reasoning is its generality. . . . Any claim that what is a reason for me is not a reason for someone else to draw the same conclusion must be backed up by further reasons, to show that this apparent deviation from generality can be accounted for in terms that are themselves general. The generality of reasons means that they apply not only in identical circumstances but also in relevantly similar circumstances—and that what counts as a relevant similarity or difference can be explained by reasons of the same generality. Ideally, the aim is to arrive at principles that are universal and exceptionless.[34]

Thus if something is a reason for drawing a certain conclusion, then reasons relevantly similar to it must support conclusions that are relevantly similar to the original one. Relevant similarity is presumably, in some sense, a matter of the original reason's and conclusion's forms rather than their particular contents. If the fact that I know something to follow from something I know is a reason to conclude that I know it too, then *anything* someone knows to follow from something he knows is something he knows too. This talk of the generality of reasoning is equivalent to talk of a fit between rules of inference and inferences governed by them, since if cogent reasoning is general in the way Nagel describes, then if R is a reason for concluding that C, we can formulate an exceptionless schematic rule of inference to the effect that from any proposition formally similar to R we may infer a conclusion formally similar to C (and given such an exceptionless rule, our reasoning that C on the basis of R is general in the intended sense).

This ideal of generality *does* govern our conception of cogent reasoning, a conception that depends, moreover, on the substantial attainment of that ideal. Yet on the account of scepticism offered in this book, it isn't completely attainable, and this way of putting the matter has a certain advantage over its formulation in terms of an equilibrium between arguments and rules of inference. That formulation speaks of the failure of a

34. Nagel, *Last Word*, 5.

purely *hypothetical* diachronic process to result in an exceptionless fit between rules of inference we treat as valid and particular inferences we find compelling. This way of putting it speaks instead of the failure of our *actual* argumentative practice to conform fully to an ideal of the generality of reasoning. This ideal both regulates and helps constitute our very conception of reasoning; but that it isn't completely attainable is, I believe, the most important moral to be drawn from a consideration of philosophical scepticism.

INDEX

Dummett, Michael, 5n, 8, 80–81, 96–97, 98, 115n

Enc, Berent, 67n
epistemological realism, 5, 7–8, 40, 79, 82–83, 95, 138
externalism, externalists, 15–16, 22, 24, 38, 115

Fitch, Frederic, 102–103
foundationalism, foundationalist, 27, 56
freedom, 9, 131, 143, 146–149, 151, 152; of the will, 150

generality, 9, 131, 152, 156–157
Gentzen, Gerhard, 121
Gettier, Edmund, 37–38
Gibbs, Benjamin, 35n
Goodman, Nelson, 3, 111, 133–134, 138

Hacking, Ian, 31–35, 40, 52
Harman, Gilbert, 16n, 41n
Hawthorne, John, 123–129
hinge propositions, 62–65
Horwich, Paul, 85n
Hume, David, 3, 110, 115

inductive inference, reasoning, 110–111, 138
inference to the best explanation, 54, 66
interior operation. See topological operations
internalism, internalists, 38, 115, 117
invariantism, 126; skeptical, 129

Jacquette, Dale, 122

Kaiser, Keith, 151n
Kant, Immanuel, 141, 147–151
Kaplan, Mark, 43n, 75n, 85n, 107n
Klein, Peter, 25, 27–28
knowledge, 4–5, 8, 18, 21–22, 29–30, 37–38, 42–44, 46, 48–49, 51, 73, 79, 84–85, 90–91, 93–94, 96, 101, 127; individual propositional knowledge, 5, 8, 18, 29–30, 38–39, 41, 44, 50–52, 79, 85, 90, 93, 105, 125; knowledge's being available, 5, 8, 39–44, 46, 48, 50–52, 82, 84, 90, 92–93, 95, 100, 102–103, 105, 116, 120–121, 125
Kripke, Saul, 16, 32, 53, 106

Leeds, Stephen, 86
Lehrer, Keith, 59
Lewis, C. I., 20, 30
Lewis, David, 69, 75, 108, 113
lotteries, lottery, 123–124, 128

McKinsey, J. C. C., 99
Malcolm, Norman, 31–32, 42, 69
modus ponens, 112, 119, 121, 122
Moore, G. E., 6, 8, 18, 31–32, 54, 57–61, 65–67, 131, 140
Moore's paradox, 47, 77, 89
moral luck, 9, 131, 143, 146

Nagel, Thomas, 143–145, 146n, 153, 156
Nozick, Robert, 14n, 16n, 34n, 55n, 75n, 108, 112–119, 120n, 121, 123

paradox(es), 2–3, 84n, 128; grue, 3, 138; Liar, 3; Russell's, 3; sorities, 141–142
possibility, possible, 4–5, 8, 17–18, 29, 31, 33, 35, 41–43, 46, 48–49, 51, 73, 79, 84–85, 91, 94, 96, 101–102, 106–108; epistemic, 5, 8, 17–18, 29–33, 35–38, 41–42, 51–52, 73, 79, 82, 91–92, 100, 102, 105, 127; logical or metaphysical, 31–32, 73, 80, 96, 102
Powers, Lawrence H., 112n
Pritchard, H. A., 43
Putnam, Hilary, 32, 81, 87n
Pyrrhonian, Pyrrhonians, 1, 4, 26, 137n

Quine, W. V., 106, 133n, 134–135, 154

Radford, Colin, 45
Rasiowa, Helena, 92n
Ramsey, F. P., 85, 87n
Rawls, John, 135
realism, realist (and antirealism), 2, 5–6, 8, 80–81, 91, 96, 98–101, 109, 141, 151. See also epistemological realism; topology, topological: realism
Reid, Thomas, 58
rule(s) of inference, 7, 9, 13–14, 84, 104, 122, 125, 129–130, 133–134, 136, 146, 152–153, 156
rule of sensitivity, 70–71, 75, 79
Russell, Bertrand, 22n, 58, 61, 63, 66

sceptical hypothesis, hypotheses, 3, 5–6, 8, 11–12, 17, 19, 50, 52, 54–57, 59–61, 64, 67–70, 82, 118, 140, 151